Celebrating the World of Work

Celebrating the World of Work

Interviews and Activities

Susan Conklin Thompson

2001
Teacher Ideas Press
A Division of
Libraries Unlimited, Inc.
Englewood, Colorado

This book is dedicated to Chelsie Hess, who can enter any career that she wants to, and to all people, everywhere, who significantly affect all our lives through their hard work and integrity.

TEACHER IDEAS PRESS
A Division of
Libraries Unlimited, Inc.
P.O. Box 6633
Englewood, CO 80155-6633
1-800-237-6124
www.lu.com/tip

Library of Congress Cataloging-in-Publication Data

Thompson, Susan Conklin.
    Celebrating the world of work : interviews and activities / Susan Conklin Thompson.
       p. cm.
    Includes bibliographical references and index.
    ISBN 1-56308-669-7 (paper)
    1. Vocational guidance--Study and teaching (Elementary)--United States. 2. Occupations--Study and teaching (Elementary)--United States. 3. Professions--Study and teaching (Elementary)--United States. I. Title.

HF5382.5.U5 T48 2001
372.14'25--dc21
                                                              2001018117

Contents

Acknowledgments

This book was a fascinating project. I thank the people who were considerate, kind, and generous with their time and talents. Thanks to Keith Thompson, William Conklin, Beth Wilkinson, Steve Welch, and each of the interesting and talented people who appear in this book. Also thanks to my editors, Susan Zernial and Rich Lane of Libraries Unlimited, who have made this book possible. Special thanks to my children, Kayenta and Rosalie, and children everywhere, who inspire us with their understanding about and interest in other people and the world.

Introduction

People everywhere are involved in jobs and careers that are not only important to them but also very important to other people and the communities in which they live. Children really enjoy learning about other people and their talents. This book is composed of people's stories about their jobs and careers, told in their own words. The stories bring the individual people and their thoughts alive for children.

The purpose of this book is to help children understand that there are many different kinds of careers and jobs and to introduce them to the people who do them. Each interview is followed by activities that children can try. The activities expand children's understanding of other people in the world and the work that they do.

Over a period of two years, I conducted many interviews for this book. The people interviewed live across the United States, from California to Maine, and in Central America and Mexico. The questions I asked them were open ended, such as, "What do you like about your job?" and "What would you like to tell children about your work?" What has fascinated me and affected my thinking is that, without exception, all the people interviewed said basically the same thing. They all commented on the integrity of their work, how they continually learn new things so they can be the best that they can be at their jobs, and that the most rewarding part of what they do is that they are able to help others and have a positive impact on their lives. Other themes mentioned include being able to be creative and to express themselves in various ways through their work.

It is important for children to know that so many people value their work and, every day, try the best that they can on their jobs. It is inspiring also to know that people everywhere are proud of their jobs and like what they do.

Celebrating the World of Work contains interesting information about a variety of people and their jobs and careers; open-ended projects; stories and recipes; many book suggestions; and numerous integrated activities that build on the children's previous experiences, help them gain new experiences, and expand their understanding of other people and the world around them. Elementary-grade students of all developmental levels will be interested in and challenged by the information in the interviews and the open-ended nature of the activities.

This book is arranged alphabetically, but you need not proceed sequentially from one section to the next. Browse through the book with the children and decide whom you would like to read about and which activities you would like to try. Some interviews and corresponding activities may fit perfectly with a unit you are involved in or a topic you are studying. The activities are integrated and are a good fit for what you are studying in different areas of learning, such as language arts, math, science, art, and social studies.

Of course, there are many other interesting occupations in addition to those included in this book. You may want to conduct some interviews of your own and design your own activities that help children learn about various careers. The children will also have ideas about people they can interview. This book is an excellent, positive beginning in introducing children to people who say "I like my job!"

Chapter 1

Anthropologist

Interview With Barbara Mueller

We learn about people in the present by studying them in the past. I have always enjoyed history and thinking about people and how they have lived. When I was in college, I took a class in anthropology that taught me about cultures. I had a chance to travel around West Germany by train, and I discovered that I love to learn about people. I want to know people and who they are, so I became an anthropologist.

Being an anthropologist can be a puzzle or a mystery. A part of anthropology is looking at remains from the past and figuring out how people lived and what their lifestyle was in a particular setting. For example, we might find a tooth and from that tooth decide what the people were eating, their diet and health, and how old they were when they died. I like to visit archeological sites to study the people and their civilizations. I have been to Mayan and Incan ruins, the pyramids in Egypt, and temples in Indonesia.

Some anthropologists study primates to figure out things about people. They observe many things about primates, such as their social habits and how they raise their young. Then the anthropologists make connections to how people lived in the prehistoric past.

I have had many fascinating experiences as an anthropologist. Once, when in China, I went to the zoo. My husband and I wanted to find the panda bears, so we followed the sign to their cage. Our bus was going to leave in 20 minutes, so we knew we would have to find our way out of the zoo quickly. There were many paths leading out of the zoo, and we did not know which one to take. We did not know how to ask anyone how to get out because the people around us were speaking Chinese and we did not know how to speak Chinese. My husband took a piece of paper, and with a pencil, wrote a symbol. He showed the symbol to a man walking by and the man pointed to the path out. I was so surprised. When I asked him how he knew that symbol, he told me that when we were on the airplane the symbol was over the door and he knew it must mean "Exit." Sometimes you just have to be clever to communicate.

Another time, we were in Hungary participating in a folk dance at a recreation center. There was a leader teaching everyone the steps. He was telling all of us to go three steps to the left and then three steps to the right. We didn't speak Hungarian, and we were going eight steps to the left and eight steps to the right!

1

To be an anthropologist, you need to know about many things, such as history, art, music, dance, psychology, and sociology, as well as several languages. A culture cannot be separated into little parts, with each part fitting together to make the whole. People need to fully understand a culture before they can be valuable participants. You have to be open minded and accept customs and traditions that are different from yours.

When we were in Hong Kong, we wanted to order food from a menu, and the menu said "chicken feet." My husband thought that it probably meant chicken thighs like we have in the United States. When the chicken came, it was in a bamboo basket. We pulled out the leg and it really was a chicken foot with toes, deep fried in fat. This is an example of a new experience in a culture different from ours. When you experience other cultures, you learn about yourself, your strengths and weaknesses and the kinds of challenges you enjoy. Because anthropologists travel a lot, they cannot be afraid of anything foreign and must realize that there will be many strange situations—change is necessary!

Exploring a Career as an Anthropologist

1. Barbara mentions commonalities and differences among cultures. To help children explore the concept of commonalities and differences, ask each child to create illustrations using crayons, paints, or pencils about something that makes him or her feel happy. Provide each child with a chance to tell about his or her picture. Then lead the children in discussing the similarities and differences between what makes each child happy. Through discussion, help the children connect this concept in a global way, building the understanding that there are both many similarities, and at the same time cultural differences, among all people wherever they live. Peter Spier's *People* (1980) contains countless small pictures of people in all parts of the world and in different historical periods and is fascinating to examine. *Material World: A Global Family Portrait,* by Peter Menzel (1994), is a fantastic photo story about families all over the world and the material possessions they have.

2. There are many excellent books to share with children about the make-up and beliefs of various families, including *All Kinds of Families,* by Norma Simon (1976); *The Trees of the Dancing Goats,* by Patricia Polacco (1996) (a sensitive story about Hanukkah); *The Old Hogan,* by Margaret Kahn Garaway (1993) (a story about a Navajo family); and *People of the Breaking Day,* by Marcia Sewall (1990) (a story of the Wampanoog people living in southeastern Massachusetts).

3. Encourage children to share experiences they have had in which things were done a little differently from the way they are in their homes. This might be as simple as noting that another family sat down for dinner or cooked their eggs differently. Help children to understand that various people like different things and that this is not good or bad, just different. Some children may be new to this country or even the school and can talk about some of the difficulties they faced coming to a new place. If English is a second language to some children, they can talk about what it is like to communicate when you do not know the language well. Aliki's (1998) wonderful *Marianthe's Story: Spoken Memories/Painted Words* tells the story of a young girl who is uprooted and encounters a new school, customs, and language. She expresses herself and tells her story through both pictures and words.

this activity to be meaningful for older children, you can create a scenario for the children to discover. For example, you can hold a candle flame under a flower pot to blacken the bottom so the pottery resembles a cooking pot. Break the blackened pot and bury the shards. Also, bury ashes from a fireplace in the sand by the pot shards. Now children can discover an old cooking pot near an ancient fireplace.

6.   Some of the most fascinating history is in our own families. Involve children in conducting oral history interviews of family members and then share the information with the group.

7.   Encourage children to read Susan Saunders's (1987) *Margaret Mead: The World Was Her Family* to learn about a famous woman anthropologist.

Chapter 2

Antiques and Flea Market Vendor

Interview With Phyllis Ernst

I remember the first auction I went to. I just went to buy some things to furnish a cabin. Before I knew it, I had bought a whole truckload of things! So then I had a garage sale to get rid of the extra stuff. I still had things left after the garage sale, so I went to a flea market and set up a table to get rid of the rest of the junk. I enjoyed it so much that now I have a business in old stuff. It took a while to learn what was junk and what was more valuable, and now I try to handle less junk and more antiques.

It's hard to make money in the antique and flea market business. Working in this business has to be a labor of love because it is hard to make money and there is a lot of competition. Also, if you don't have a shop in which to put your junk, storage is a problem because the stuff really clutters up your house. If you can stand the competition and the junk all around you, then this is a fascinating job.

Really, the antique and flea market business is just a big treasure hunt. I have had to learn a great deal about the value and quality of collectibles. I hunt all around to buy things cheaply and then sell them for more money. Some of the furniture I repair to resell, but most I just sell as-is. If you can focus on collecting and selling just a few kinds of items, you can learn a lot about them. For example, some people deal in just quilts, jewelry, or dishes. Then they have time to research the history and kinds of each.

Even if something is old, it may not be very valuable if it is not in good condition. Condition is everything in terms of value. You have to be very honest when you buy and sell things. If someone doesn't know what an item is worth, you need to be fair while at the same time making a little money.

The antique and flea market business is more than buying and selling. You can learn a lot about history and about many different people. That is what keeps it so interesting.

Exploring a Career as an Antiques and Flea Market Vendor

1. Have several antique items available for the children to examine, or have them bring items from home. Involve them in selecting an item and learning about its history. What time period is the item from? What was it used for?

2. Read Mitsumasa Anno's (1984) *Anno's Flea Market* to the children. On a long piece of butcher paper, have the children draw open shops similar to those illustrated in the book. Which kinds of merchandise will be in their shops? With the children, brainstorm categories of objects people collect and sell, such as buttons and jewelry.

3. Outdoor flea markets are similar to other outdoor markets such as craft markets and farmers' markets. Outdoor markets from all over the world are described in Ted Lewin's (1996) *Market* How many children in your group have been to an outdoor market? How would they describe the experience? Some children may have sold things at a family garage sale, which is really a flea market of their own. Read the following story about a trunk to the children. Then, lead them in discussing things they collect, garage sales they have had or attended, and antiques that are in their families.

The Trunk

Rosy wanted an old, antique trunk. She had wanted a trunk for eight years, ever since her mother told her about the antique trunk she got from her mother when she graduated from high school. Rosy's mother's trunk sat in the guest room at their house and held special things from her mother's life: old letters, quilts she collected, and souvenirs from her wedding.

When Rosy was four years old, her mother opened the trunk and showed her what she had collected over the years. Many times since then, Rosy asked her mother whether she could look through the old trunk again, and her mother always helped with the looking, carefully unwrapping old things and placing them in Rosy's hands.

Rosy had a collection of her own. She had an old doll from her great-grandmother, a special ring from her friend Sarah, a stuffed animal she won at a carnival by throwing balls into slots with different points above them, greeting cards she had received from her family and friends at Christmas and her birthday, and a small replica of the Statue of Liberty that her grandfather brought back to her when he went to New York City on a business trip. Rosy just needed a trunk of her own in which to put her collection.

There were two antique stores in town. Rosy's mom took her to both of them on Saturday. The first antique store was in an old building that looked to Rosy like the oldest antique of all. The roof looked as though it might fall in during a strong hailstorm like the one they had experienced last summer, when the hail was almost as big as her little brother's fist. The place had a funny smell like her aunt's old basement, and Rosy had trouble walking around in the store because there were so many antiques crammed into the small space. Rosy's mom found a cup and saucer she wanted to buy, and Rosy saw lots of interesting things, including an old pair of snowshoes and a wood stove, but no trunk.

At the second antique store, there were many separate shops inside one big building. Rosy's mom told her that it was an antique mall where people brought their antiques to sell and then rented a small space for their items. When an item was sold, some of the money went to the people who had rented out the spaces to sellers. Rosy's mom bought an old quilt that was white, lavender, and yellow. She showed Rosy how the quilt had pointed pieces of fabric along one end and told her that these points were called prairie points. Although Rosy looked carefully through every area, she did not find a trunk.

On the way back to the house, she talked with her mom about where else they could look for a trunk. They turned onto a side street and saw many cars parked on one side and people walking on the sidewalk and in the yard in front of a large, old house. "A garage sale!" exclaimed Rosy's mother. She loved to go to garage sales and browse around, even though she rarely bought anything. "Let's stop," she said.

They parked the car and got out. It was crowded at the sale. There were many people on the front lawn looking at old toys, clothing, and furniture. There was also a lot of old junk in a large garage and in the backyard. Rosy looked around in the garage. She saw jars of old buttons on shelves, rusty tools along the back wall, a few broken toys in one corner, and in the back, behind a rack of old coats, she found a trunk. It was brown with leather straps and just a little smaller than her mom's. Right then, her mom came up to see what she had found. "It's a trunk, Mom!" said Rosy, excitedly. Her mom looked at the trunk and told her that it was an old camelback trunk, which is one that has a rounded top. The top creaked as they opened it, and their hands got dusty. Inside the trunk, there was a shelf. The inside of the trunk and the shelf were covered with an old fabric.

"How much does the trunk cost?" asked Rosy's mom. Rosy found a sticker inside the lid that denoted $40.00. "That's a good price for a trunk like this, and you will still have $10.00 left to buy something else or to save for another time," her mom told her. Together they lifted the trunk and carried it to the lady taking money, who was sitting at a card table on the front lawn. Rosy was very excited with her find and couldn't wait to get the trunk home and put her collection on the fabric-covered shelf. What she didn't know then was that someday she would be showing her own daughter and son her collection in this very same old trunk.

Chapter 3

Architect

Interview With
Annette Renner-Richter

This is a drawing of my office building in Boston, Massachusetts. I have wanted to be an architect since I was 14. As an architect, I get to create space, bring my ideas to reality, and try out many new materials. I love to draw, and my drawings turn out to be a finished building that people get to see and go into.

Architects don't earn a lot of money unless they are designing something someone will pay a lot for. One thing that is hard about being an architect is that even if I don't like what is being designed, I have to develop it anyway. People come to me and tell me what they need and some of their ideas for a building they want me to design, and then I create lots of sketches of the building using their ideas. I build a model building resembling a small dollhouse or building for small figures. After my colleagues and I decide that we want to create the building like the model, we draw a sketch of the building's plans, adding elevations and perspective views. We meet with the client (the person who wanted the building built) and get his or her approval. We add more details to the drawing and then send it to the structural and mechanical engineers for them to add other details such as foundations and plumbing. After we receive the engineers' feedback regarding the requirements that need to be adhered to, we can finish the design and then build the new building.

Architecture is a very interesting field, and there are always new things to learn. I studied interior architecture in Maine, Germany. It's important to keep up on what is new. For example, there is a new development in architecture to build more low-energy houses, such as those that catch and store heat from the sunlight in winter. These houses keep the sunlight out in the summer to keep the interior cool. Houses like these will help save our natural resources and reduce consumption of energy.

Exploring a Career as an Architect

1. Talk with children about various architectural styles of buildings erected during different periods in history (see Blumenson, 1977). Take the children on a walking tour of the architecture in your community. Ahead of time, prepare a short booklet for each child with some information about the buildings you will be walking (or driving) by. Leave enough space between building-information sections for children to sketch the buildings that they see. After the field trip, engage them in talking about their observations. For example, a page of the booklet might begin with "The Old Stone Methodist Church was built in the 1700s and was the first church in the city built from stones." *A Building on Your Street,* by Seymour Simon (1973), can help children make new observations about buildings they see every day.

2. Have the children create a mural or large scrapbook of housing and other building designs by cutting pictures out of magazines, housing ads in newspapers, and realty guides. Discuss the different designs with the children, and see if all of you can guess when the structures were built. As you become more familiar with some common architectural features of different decades, this will become much easier. For example, the Queen Anne style, with its towers, turrets, and tall chimneys, was popular between 1880 and 1900, and the Gothic Revival style, with steeply pitched roofs, gingerbread trim, and gable edges, was popular between 1830 and 1860.

3. An excellent pictorial guide to American architecture is John J.-G. Blumenson's (1977) *Identifying American Architecture.* It is a small book that contains illustrations of various houses from many different time periods.

4. After studying many designs through reading and on the architectural tour, challenge children to design houses and public buildings of their own. They should design them on sheets of paper, and depending on their developmental level, create 3-D models using cardboard, boxes, wood, or even gingerbread. This would be a wonderful time to have an architect as a guest to talk about space considerations: how big bathrooms and bedrooms are, where closets are located, how much space is allowed for hallways, and what these rooms and spaces actually look like on blueprint paper.

5. It is important for children to realize that some buildings are more energy efficient than others. Encourage them to look around their school or library. Is the building energy efficient? In what ways? Are the windows large or small? Point out that large windows may be efficient if they are facing south so the sun heats the rooms but may not be efficient if they do not. Introduce them to various building materials that people use. Straw bales, adobe, and tires are all considered energy efficient. Wood houses are more difficult to heat. Some flooring has hot water heat built in. Encourage the children to research what causes some buildings to be more energy efficient than others.

Chapter 4

Art Teacher

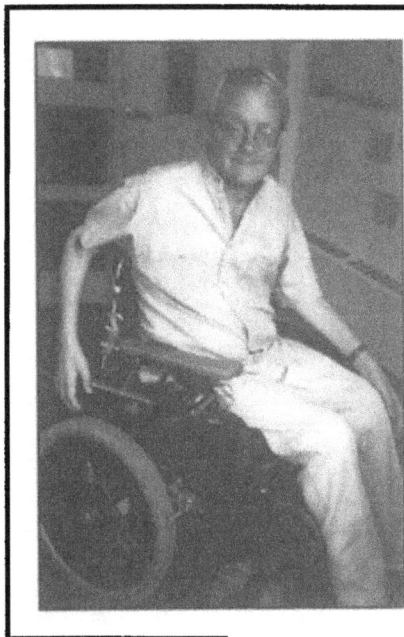

Interview With Steve Welch

When I was eight years old, I decided I wanted to be an artist. A friend who lived next door to me drew a picture for me of a spaceman, and I thought that was pretty neat. After that, I started to draw. As I grew older, I wanted to share what I knew with other people, and I wanted them to have as much fun with art as I was having. People would watch me draw and want to know how to do what I did, and I helped them learn to draw, too.

Being an art teacher is a wonderful job. I get to be creative and to help children explore with paints, pencils, clay, and anything we can find to make interesting pictures and sculptures. It's rewarding to watch children develop their ideas and to understand that they view the world differently than I do. It's also fun to see children produce something they will be proud of for the rest of their lives.

Painting is my favorite thing in art to teach because I like to see what the colors do. It is easier to make things up, and if you don't like what you paint, you can wipe it away. You can envision a fantasy world and then actually paint it on paper. You can also play with the paint strokes and have fun with color. For example, you can paint a spot of red beside a spot of blue, and when you step back it looks like purple.

Some art teachers learn how to teach art by taking art classes in school. This also gives them a chance to talk and learn with other artists. Other art teachers just have a lot of experience with art and special talents they want to share. If you want to learn more about art, it would be a good idea to go to museums to look at artwork and to read and look at different art books so you can learn about art, other artists, and their ideas.

Exploring a Career as an Art Teacher

1. Try Steve's idea of painting a red spot next to a blue spot. What happens? Involve children in trying other colors together. What do they discover?

2. The children will enjoy experimenting with color by painting different colors on white paper. Challenge them to paint an entire sheet of paper so it looks like the sky on a stormy day, a sunset on a summer evening, or sand at a beach. How about the color of their favorite animal? The different shades of yellow or blue? The color of a bunch

of grapes? A basketful of apples? The painted pages of color can be saved for the backgrounds of their illustrations or for collages. If a child tears out a shape from a painted page, there will be an interesting texture and outline of white around the shape's edges that will enhance the collage's appearance.

3. There are many wonderful books about art written for children. A series by Colleen Carroll, which includes *How Artists See People: Boy Girl Man Woman* (1996) and *How Artists See Weather: Sun Wind Snow Rain* (1996), helps children see the world in interesting and creative ways. There are also many good children's books on specific artists, such as *My Name Is Georgia* (about Georgia O'Keefe), by Jeanette Winter (1998).

4. Ask the children what they would like to learn about art if they could learn something new. Some children will want to learn about an artist, others how to sculpt or how to draw using more perspective. Find an artist who will volunteer some time to come and help children work on specific interests, or refer the children to a good resource in a local library. Also, talk with them about what expertise they have in art and what they could teach each other. Would members of their families be willing to teach others?

5. Below and to the right is a graphic of Steve's logo. Ask the children if they can find two ink pens and a paint brush in the logo. Involve them in designing a logo of their own. What do their logos reveal about them?

6. Involve children in reading books (written for children) about master artists, such as *Van Gogh,* by Mike Venezia (1988), or *Frederic Remington,* by Ernest Rabott (1988). Also, books about artists that contain beautiful prints of various master artists' work can often be purchased inexpensively at discount stores. Involve children in painting a picture using the same technique as a particular artist. For example, Van Gogh is well known for painting pictures using short strokes and thick paint. Using finger paint or other thick paint, they can paint a vase of flowers (from a still life) or other scene, by making short strokes with a paint brush. Or the children may want to paint themes similar to those of a particular artist, such as desert objects like the ones Georgia O'Keefe painted, or the lily ponds painted by Monet.

7. Some artists paint or tattoo art on people's bodies. Show the children the following photograph of Karol Griffin, a tattoo artist, and Kayenta Nicole, who pierces people's ears. Then share the information about them with the children.

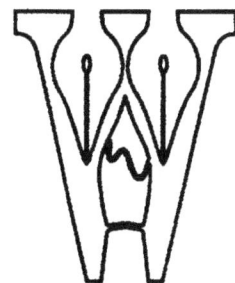

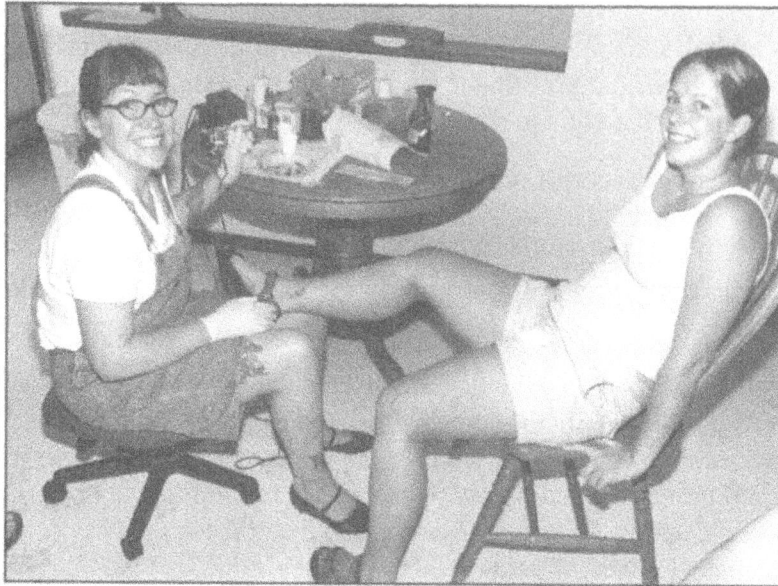

Karol Griffin and Kayenta Nicole: Tattoo Artist and Ear Piercer

Karol Griffin is a tattoo artist. She always liked to paint, draw, and take photographs. When she was in her twenties she apprenticed with a master tattoo artist to learn how to put tattoos on people. For three months before she ever tried a tattoo, Karol watched the master tattoo artist work, mixed colors of dye for the tattoos, and worked on designs.

Karol practiced putting tattoos on grapefruit and bananas before she felt ready to put one on a person. The first real tattoo she applied was on her own leg.

When people are interested in getting a tattoo, Karol tells them to think carefully about what design represents them well. Their tattoo will be a permanent part of their lives and should be an expression of who they are.

Karol does not put tattoos on anyone under 18 years old without permission from the person's parents or other guardian. She works in her home, so the atmosphere is friendly. It does hurt to have a tattoo put on your body, but it helps when it's done in a nice person's kitchen. Karol feels bad when she sees people select designs that she does not think they will like when they are older. She feels that the best part of putting on a tattoo is to watch the design move on the skin because, to her, it looks incredible.

The other young woman in the photograph with Karol is Kayenta Nicole who sells jewelry and pierces ears in a shop at a mall. She enjoys talking with the adults and children she meets, and she finds piercing people's ears to be interesting.

Many children and adults have their ears pierced. Children need adult permission if they are under 18. In many cities, there are shops where people pierce ears and put on tattoos in the same shop. For more information on piercing and tattooing, children can read Beth Wilkinson's (1998) *Coping with the Dangers of Tattooing, Body Piercing, and Branding*.

8. Many types of artists are often teachers. Besides art teachers, what other kinds of teachers are there? What knowledge do the children possess to teach others? Compile the information into a book of "resource children" for other children to use.

Chapter 5

Baker

Interview With Jean Schieck

When I was a girl, growing up, I never baked much. I was not a bread maker at home. Baking is something you cannot learn without doing. You learn the "feel" of the dough and when it is just right: too much flour or too little—how it feels and how it looks in the bowl.

I am the head baker for our school district. At 5:15 A.M., I begin making a big batch of dough for the breads that children at many different schools will eat for breakfast and lunch. I can use the same dough recipe and just make simple changes to make cinnamon rolls, maple bars, Indian fry bread, rolls for sandwiches, dinner rolls, and French bread.

My cinnamon rolls are everyone's favorite. I roll the dough out into a large rectangle on a five-foot-long table. Then I put butter and cinnamon sugar on top of the dough. Carefully, I roll the dough into a giant Tootsie-roll™ shape. Using two fingers, I measure the roll into small sections and cut them into small square shapes. Then I tuck in the ends of the roll and pinch them under. My hands get tired because on many mornings I make 1,300 rolls and have to cut, tuck, and pinch each one. Then I lay every roll on a large tray and let it rise. The instant yeast helps it rise quickly, and this step takes only about 45 minutes. After the rolls are baked, I frost each one. It takes about 20 pounds of powdered sugar for one batch of frosting. I add butter, water, and vanilla to the powdered sugar and then mix it until it is easy to spread. Then I place the rolls into boxes to be delivered to the different schools.

It's easier to plan menus for the entire month than to plan for one day at a time. The hardest part of my job is that I have to work quickly; I begin mixing the dough at 5:15 and the rolls must be finished and in the boxes by 9:00. It's very hard to get them ready so fast, and I am on my feet for at least four hours at a time while I am working. Also, being a baker is very heavy work. The sacks of flour weigh 50 pounds, and my arms get tired lifting the heavy sacks. The trays full of rolls weigh at least 35 pounds, and that's a lot of weight to lift in and out of the oven. Pinching all the rolls every morning is also hard on my fingers and arms.

To be a baker you need to like to cook. When I first started, I was scared to death that I'd forget how to make dough. I brought my own recipe to work, and at first the dough didn't look like it was turning out right, but I kept at it and the rolls were very good. After that first morning, I just kept getting better and faster at making rolls.

Boys and girls come through the kitchen and watch me bake. They like to see the big, long roll of dough, how I cut it into two-finger pieces, and how I frost the baked rolls. It makes me feel good to hear and see how much they enjoy what I bake.

My roll recipe is

Rolls

1 cup shortening, melted	1 cup powdered milk
2 cups sugar	1/8 cup salt
1 gal water, very warm	3/4 cup instant yeast
10 lbs flour	

Directions: Mix flour, sugar, powdered milk, salt, and yeast in large bowl. Add warm water and melted shortening. Mix until smooth. Add a little extra flour until dough is no longer sticky and can be handled easily. For dinner rolls, pour a little melted butter on top of dough and let rise until double in size. Roll dough out onto a lightly floured counter into a large rectangle. Starting at one end, roll the dough into a large roll. With a knife, cut the dough into pieces the size of two of your fingers. Place rolls onto cookie sheet and let rise for 25 minutes. Bake at 350 degrees for 25 minutes.

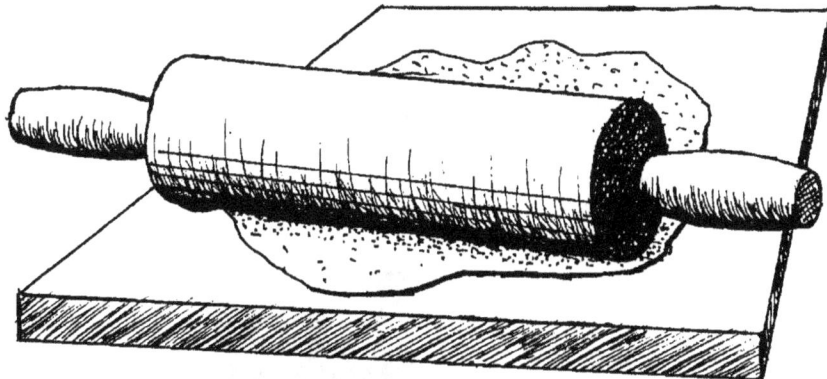

Exploring a Career as a Baker

1. What do children like to bake? Have them bring in recipes and samples of their baked goods. Using a simple graph, chart what types of bakery goods children enjoy. Make copies of the recipes for the children and help them construct books filled with recipes to be tried at home.

2. Examine a recipe with the children. How much larger would the amounts for each ingredient have to be to make enough to serve 1,000 people? This can provide a good math challenge and help them better understand the large amounts of ingredients that Jean works with every day.

3. Homemade bread is wonderful to make, smell, and eat. Bake bread with the children and involve them in the mixing of ingredients, kneading, and baking. What does the texture feel like? How do you think Jean likes the dough to feel before she bakes the bread? They can use Jean's roll recipe or another one from a book. How can you adapt the recipe for cinnamon rolls? Ask the children what other recipes they can create using Jean's basic roll dough.

4. There are many excellent children's cookbooks that clearly explain steps for baking. One with a charming twist is *Clever Cooks: A Concoction of Stories, Charms, Recipes and Riddles,* compiled by Ellin Greene (1973).

5. Bakers are all around. Involve the children in brainstorming all the places in their community that hire bakers, such as hospitals, grocery stores, pizza shops, and schools. Take a field trip to any bakery to watch bakers making rolls, pizzas, and other baked goods. Compare newly gained information to that provided in the interview with Jean. What is it about the various bakers' jobs that is the same, and what is different? Eric Carle's (1972) beautifully illustrated *Walter the Baker* is a fun story for children about a baker.

Chapter 6

Batiker of Mayan Gods

Interview With Victor Rivas Palomo

I live in a jungle in Mexico in a Mayan village called Cobá. The Mayan village is near the ancient Mayan ruin of Cobá, which was home to some 40,000 Mayans between A.D. 600 and 900. To get to my village, a traveler has to drive many miles on a road through the jungle. All through the jungle, there are small Mayan houses with thatched roofs. There is a sign on the way to the village, asking people to protect our jungles.

When I was younger, I used to be a sailor. I would take people by boat to Isla Mujeres, which means Island of Women. Many tourists visit this island each year to snorkel, have fun, and see the remains of an ancient temple.

For the last 10 years, I have been a batiker. A batiker is someone who creates pictures on fabric using wax and dye. Each morning, I ride my bike to work, which is a small hut with a grass roof. I create batik pictures from early in the morning until about 5:00 in the afternoon. I learned how to batik from a friend of mine, and I've gotten very good over the years. Batiking is a lot of work, but I like working with the wax, and the colors are very beautiful.

Most of my batik designs are of ancient Mayan gods. There is an old story that goes with each god. For example, the Mayan god with the snake (see the picture on next page) is the god of the wind. I have heard these stories since I was a young boy. My favorite design is one with the sun and moon.

Batiking is a very nice technique to learn. To create a batik picture, I use beeswax to paint a design on a piece of fabric. Then I paint the fabric with dye. Some people dip the entire fabric into the dye, but I can control the design better by painting the dye onto the fabric with a brush. The dye does not go through the wax. Every place there is wax, there are crinkly lines of color but the white parts of the fabric remain. Then I boil the wax out of the fabric by placing it in a pot of boiling water.

Batiked fabric is beautiful. Once you learn to batik, you can create fabrics to make into clothes, or you can sell batiks to make a living. I am able to support my family by selling my batik wall hangings to many tourists who come to Cobá to visit the Cobá ruins.

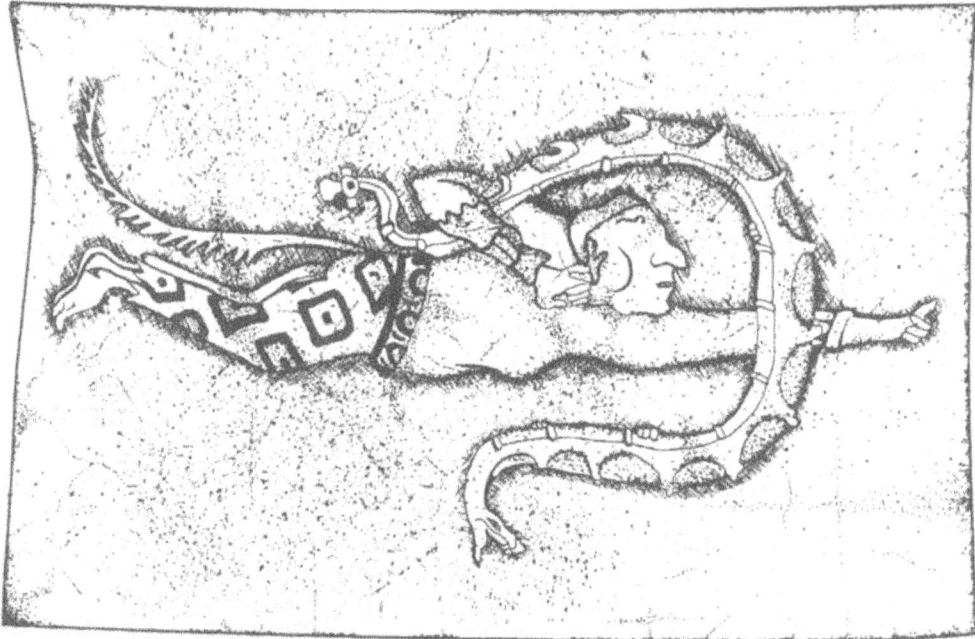

Exploring a Career as a Batiker

1. Locate Cobá on a map. It is southwest of Cancún, Mexico. Tell the children that the Mayan Indians were the first people to live in this part of Mexico. Show them a picture of an ancient Mayan ruin and talk with them about the remaining buildings. A simple Mayan temple can be replicated by placing different sizes of boxes on top of each other, with the widest box on the bottom, the next largest on top of that, and so on.

2. Involve the children in coloring fabric using the batik technique. They should begin by planning a design and drawing it with pencil on fabric. They should then paint melted paraffin or beeswax onto the fabric. (Be sure to caution them about working with warm materials.) Next they will paint dye on the fabric or crumple the fabric into a ball and dip it into the dye. They should then rinse the fabric in cold water and hang it up to dry. When the fabric is dry, the children should remove the wax by placing a brown paper bag over the fabric, then ironing over the top of the bag. (Remind them about being careful when using an iron.) The bag should be replaced with others until no more wax is picked up with the heat. For additional information on batiking and other methods of coloring fabric, see Susan Conklin Thompson's (1998) *Folk Art Tells a Story: An Activity Guide.* Beryl Martin's (1971) *Batik for Beginners* is also a good guide. For fascinating information on many old crafts, see *World Crafts: A Celebration of Designs and Skills,* by Jacqueline Herald (1992).

3. Using crayons, children can create Mayan or other designs of their own on paper. They can use the same batik concept of wax resisting paint by coloring their design with crayons and then painting with watercolors over the crayons. Allow time for sharing their designs and exploring their reactions to the crayon-resist technique.

4. Talk with the children about the need to preserve the jungle. The sign in the jungle by Victor's house reads: "The Jungle Is Life. Avoid Burning It." Each year, more and more of the jungle is intentionally burned to clear land for farming. When the jungle is burned, much of the wildlife is destroyed. Many people are worried that in the future there will not be any more jungle lands and the jungle wildlife will be extinct.

5. Let the children examine the illustration of a Mayan house in the jungle. How might life in a grass Mayan hut in the jungle be different from the life the children lead? How might the temperature, the wildlife, the villages, the water supply, and material possessions be different from what they know now?

Chapter 7

Beautician

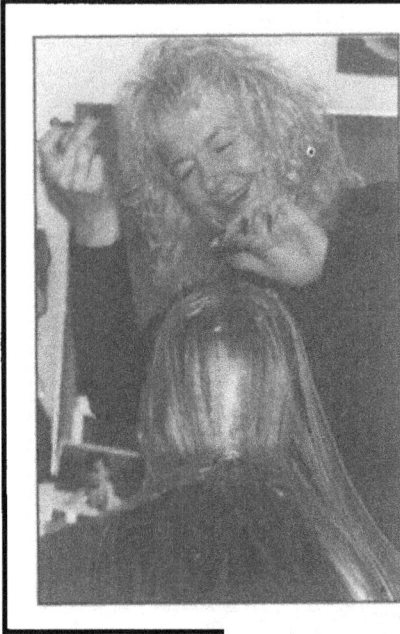

Interview With Carole Gording

When I was a little girl, my sister would love to fix my hair. She would see a style she wanted for herself and then would fix my hair in that style. She came up with some very interesting hair styles for me. I decided that I would like to do hair and learn how to do it the right way. To learn how to be a beautician, I went to a special beauty school in Canada.

Being a beautician is a wonderful job because I can make people feel better about themselves by helping them look better. Friends like to have their hair fixed, and it makes them feel good. I started cutting hair at home, and then I bought my own shop. I really like the people who come into my shop. They tell me interesting things about themselves and their families, and I get to know them very well. I also get to be very creative as I cut hair into different styles; experiment with permanents; and dye hair black, blonde, red, and brown. Once a boy wanted me to dye his hair blonde with orange ends, and it turned out very well. There are many times when people don't know what they want to do with their hair, and I can figure it out for them.

If I have a lot of customers, I am busy all the time. But I don't have to work all the time if I don't want to—I choose my own hours. I am on my feet all day long and moving around a lot, so it is good exercise. Also, I can keep up on what is new by going to interesting training sessions to learn new things about hair products, styles, and hair care. Then I can share what I learn with other people. For example, if boys and girls go swimming, they should wash their hair with a special shampoo for getting the chlorine out before it dries. Chlorine crystallizes on the hair as it dries, and it changes the texture and color of the hair.

I recently moved into a new shop. The old shop was getting too small for my business. My new shop is roomy, and there is much more space for all the girls who fix hair and do fingernails.

Exploring a Career as a Beautician

1. Talk with children about hair care. Beauticians can be very helpful in providing advice on how to keep hair healthy. A good beautician can talk with children about shampoos that are healthful for hair, conditioners, how often to shampoo hair, when to get a trim, and so forth. *Brush up on Hair Care,* by Betty Lou Phillips (1982), is useful for helping children think about how to care for their hair.

2. It's fun to think of a variety of hair styles and colors. Children can clip hair styles out of magazines and make posters of different styles and colors. Do they see trends in styles from different time periods? How about color trends? Which hair styles do they think will define the twenty-first century?

3. Challenge children to pretend that they are setting a new trend in style and color. They can design the styles by drawing or painting them on paper. Have a "style" show with the finished styles, encouraging children to explain their creations.

4. Many beauticians also fix fingernails. It would be helpful to have a beautician demonstrate nail care and how to carefully polish nails. Nails can have a variety of designs such as spots, bugs, or even holiday symbols such as Christmas wreaths or Valentine's Day hearts, painted on top of a color. Klutz's (1997) *Nail Art* provides wonderful ideas for different designs for nails. Challenge children to create their own designs and illustrate them on paper. They can trace around their hands and then paint or color each drawn fingernail with a different design.

5. Throughout history, people have done some wonderful things with hair and wigs. Lead children in researching hair from centuries past and the place it held in society. For example, in the 1800s, the aristocrats wore puffy, white wigs, men and women alike. Explain to them that if they were designing costumes for plays and movies or fixing actors' hair for specific parts, they would have to be historical hair experts. Have each child or group of children select a play or book and design costumes and hair styles for each character.

6.   What kind of questions do people ask beauticians? What do the beauticians have to know to answer so many different questions? Children will be interested in knowing that people ask beauticians many things about hair and nail care—everything from which glues work to stick on fake fingernails to what to do when the store dye has colored their hair green! Also, people tell their beauticians many things about themselves, so beauticians have to be good listeners and really enjoy being with people.

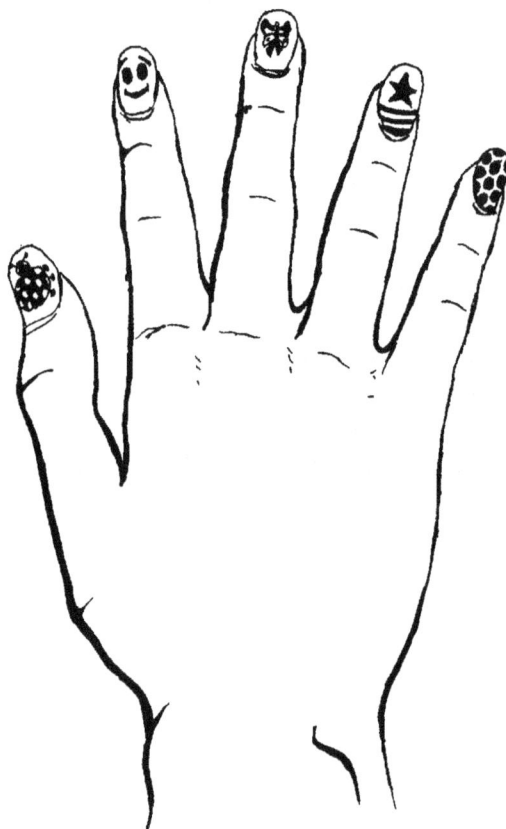

Chapter 8

Biomedical Equipment Technician

Interview With Chris D'Arrezo

It is very fun to assess a problem and then correct it. I like to fix things and to find out what a machine that is not working is supposed to do. Then I try to fix it so it does what it's supposed to do. When I first started fixing machines, I was testing people's hearing, and I was good at keeping the audiometers running. When I realized that I liked to fix electronic equipment, I wanted to learn all I could about electronics, so I went to college and completed a degree in electronics.

Now I work in a hospital and am responsible for many things. I take care of a large variety of medical equipment. Sometimes I don't even know how to turn on a piece of equipment, and I have to learn how to fix it. This is fun because it is a real challenge. I also take care of all the medical equipment, perform preventive maintenance and electrical safety inspections, and look after other types of equipment like television sets and paging systems.

Some of the machines I look after monitor patients, and some machines treat patients. Some of the machines are very important to keeping patients alive. It's up to me to make sure the equipment works so the patients will live, which is a tremendous responsibility. Because of the importance of my job, I need to know about many things, and my college degree helps out a lot. When I went to school, I studied electronics, electrical circuits, chemistry, hydraulics, physics, and biology.

I like to keep people happy. If I can fix a machine and help a caregiver or a patient, then I am happy. And at the same time, I have a lot of fun with the machines that I work with.

Exploring a Career as an Equipment Technician

1. Talk with children about different kinds of machines. *Machines at Work,* by Alan Ward (1993), shows basic principles of machines and simple activities to try out machine concepts. Ask where they have seen simple and complex machines at school and at home. What machines have they seen that perform fascinating jobs? Examples they may mention are a donut maker, which puts in the dough, flips the donuts as they cook,

and then drops them into a section to cool; a machine that wraps candy kisses; or the robots in Bob Haus's car factory (see interview in Chapter 10).

2. Hold a "machine day" to examine machines that are common in the children's lives. Ask each child to bring a machine from home for the group to examine. The machine may be as simple as a can opener or more complex, like a bread machine. As a group, talk about the uses of the various machines. Encourage the children to speculate about how some of the more complicated machines work. The speculation will help expand their thinking and need not be scientifically correct. The children should also keep a record for several days of all the machines they observe and use. What are the machines, and what would happen if these machines quit working? Are some more necessary than others? How would a day without machines change their lives? They will probably enjoy thinking about a day without cars, refrigerators, and other machines.

3. Nurture the children's inventive spirit by challenging them to design a new machine that performs some amazing task. Let them illustrate their machines on large pieces of butcher paper or drawing paper, using crayons or markers. Display the machine illustrations and let each child tell about his or her incredible machine.

4. Have several machines available for children to take apart, such as alarm clocks, toasters, and irons. What do the insides look like? Can they draw a picture of the machine and the individual parts that they remove? What are the parts called?

5. Challenge them to put back together a machine that they have taken apart. Those who are mechanical will be able not only to take something apart and put it back together, but also see what is wrong with it if there is a problem. Provide them with opportunities to share and discuss the process of taking the machine apart and the challenge of putting all the parts back where they belong.

6. Some children will be fascinated with taking some old machines and combining them to create a new machine. Encourage them to use their inventive spirit; provide them with basic tools such as hammers, screwdrivers, and pliers; and let them create something new.

7. Throughout history there have been people who specialize in fixing things other than machines, such as shoes. Many children will be surprised that people used to fix boots and shoes so they could be worn longer. Explain that there is not as great a tendency for people in the United States to fix lots of things today as there was in the past because it is now easier (and affordable) to throw things away and buy new ones.

Chapter 9

Candy Store Clerk

Interview With Rita Sweeney

I'm 80 years old, and all my life I've lived in Salem, Massachusetts. When I was younger, I was a secretary, and after my children were raised, I started to work in a candy store with a friend of mine. The candy store closed, and I began to work in the candy store I work in now, Ye Olde Pepper Companie.

It's a lot of fun to work in a candy shop, waiting on customers, helping them select candy, giving change, and making sure the store gets the correct amount of money. Many pleasant people come into the store. Salem is a tourist town because of the witch trials and its historical buildings. The House of the Seven Gables, which Nathaniel Hawthorne's book was based on, is right across the street. The tourists who come into our shop are visiting from all over the world, and we hear many languages. My mother was French, and I speak French; another girl in the shop speaks Italian; and another is Polish.

We make most of the candy we sell right in the shop. The hard candy and chocolate are ours, and my favorites are the chocolate-covered nuts and caramels. The shop always smells good and looks pretty with all the jars and candies. Our shop is famous for its Salem Gibralters. The Gibralters are the oldest commercially made and packaged candy in America. They taste like sugary mints. They were first made by the Spencer family, who lost everything they owned on a trip to America from England. They came to live in Salem, and it was known that Mrs. Spencer made candy, so a barrel of sugar was given to her and she made candy and began the business. She drove a wagon all over selling her candy.

The people who work in our shop, and the owners, are all very nice to work with. If I am sick or cannot come in, they will arrange for another lady to work for me. I am one of the younger sales clerks—one lady is 82. The cash register was easy to learn how to work when I came to the shop, and the owners helped me learn how to pack the chocolates for the customers who want them in boxes. Other customers pick individual chocolates from the glass cases, and we weigh them and wrap them up. It was not hard to learn how to interact with the customers because we talk to people in the store the same way you talk to friends you meet on the street.

My granddaughter is a tour guide in The House of the Seven Gables across the street. She works weekends and summers. To be a tour guide, you have to learn a lot of history about the place you are telling people about, because people ask many questions when you are taking them through. You have to be at least in high school to be hired. My daughters were tour guides in a historical witch house when they were younger.

Because I am older, I only work a few days a week. I like to stay active, and I really enjoy getting out of the house and meeting interesting people from all around. Anyone who would like to try Salem Gibralters can order them at:

> Ye Olde Pepper Companie
> 122 Derby Street
> Salem, MA 01970
> Telephone: 978-745-2744

Exploring a Career as a Candy Store Clerk

1. Children will enjoy setting up a store in the room, pricing the items for sale, and paying for them with play money. Giving change is good practice for understanding and working with money.

2. While children interact, have them talk with one another as they would if they really were store workers and customers. How do you ask politely what something costs or where something is located? How do you make pleasant conversation about the weather or where someone lives?

3. Rita has to weigh the candy for her customers. Have a balance beam or candy scale available for the children to use and small plastic bags containing candy (made from the recipe on the next page) or other small edible items. Let the children practice weighing a bag on the scale and reporting the weight. Can they take empty bags and fill them with flour, rice, candy, or supplies to fulfill a customer's order for a specific amount?

4. The candy store Rita works in makes candy in a room next to the store. With the children, make a batch of candy using the following recipe. The children may also want to try a favorite candy recipe from home.

> *Cut Glass Hard Candy* (makes 2 1/4 lbs)
> 1/2 cup confectioner's sugar
> 3 3/4 cups sugar
> 1 1/2 cups light corn syrup
> 1 cup water
> 1 tsp flavoring oil
> 1/2 tsp food coloring

Directions: Sprinkle a 12-inch-by-24-inch strip of heavy-duty aluminum foil with the confectioner's sugar. Mix the next three ingredients in a large, heavy saucepan. Stir over medium heat until the sugar dissolves. Boil, without stirring, until the temperature reaches 310 degrees F, or until drops of syrup form hard and brittle threads in cold water. Remove the pan from the heat. Stir in flavoring oil and food coloring. Pour the candy onto the foil. Cool; immediately break into pieces or cut with household shears. Store in airtight containers.

5. The House of the Seven Gables, where Rita's granddaughter works, is famous because of Nathaniel Hawthorne's book by the same name. Explain to the children that a gable is a peak in the roof of the house and show them the following picture.

Feathertop is one of Hawthorne's stories that has been adapted into picture book form by Robert D. San Souci (1992). Children will enjoy the colorful illustrations and the story of the pumpkin head scarecrow that comes to life.

6. A candy store is only one type of store that children will be interested in learning about. Ask them about the wide variety of stores that contribute to a community. In what store would they most be interested in working as a clerk? *Stores,* by Alvin Schwartz (1977), takes children on a tour of a large variety of stores.

Chapter 10

Car Factory Worker and Train Engineer

Interview With Bob Haus

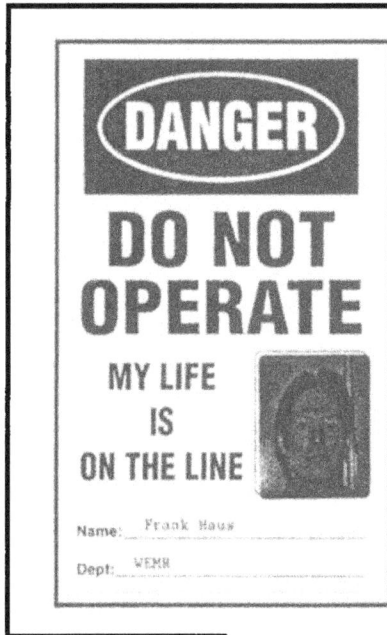

I used to be a train engineer before I went to work in a car factory. I was in control of the entire train. The trains I drove shipped everything from soup to steel. It was a great job. I got to spend my time outdoors, and people would wave to us as we went by.

As an engineer, I worked in the yard, where we would inspect the locomotive to see that it was ready for work. The oil had to be checked, and we had to make sure that the generator was working well. We would wait for the conductor, who told us when to go and what to do. The conductor would have a list from the yardmaster, and he would work with the brakemen to switch the cars. They would sort the train cars like a postal worker does letters, onto different tracks to become a train. The brakemen would walk the tracks and give hand signals to the engineers. There are different hand signals. One tells the engineer to stop and another to slow down because of other cars on the tracks.

I also worked the road, which means I drove the train from Pittsburgh, Pennsylvania, to Youngstown, Ohio, which is about 52 miles. The train line I worked for was the PLE, which stands for Pittsburgh and Lake Erie. The hard part of the job was that I was always on call, and I never knew when I was going to work when working the road.

I learned how to be an engineer on the job from another engineer. The railroad hired us on as firemen when there used to be steam engines. The firemen fed the fire with coal, and then, when the engines went to diesel fuel, the firemen became apprentice engineers. We also had to pass a road and rules test to make sure we knew how to do the job and knew about all the safety considerations.

Sometimes there were accidents on the job. People driving cars or walking should be very careful crossing railroad tracks. There are times when cars speed up to go across crossings and try to beat the trains. This is very dangerous, and the people in the cars can be killed. Also, sometimes our train cars would derail. There is a 3/4-inch flange on each train wheel, and that is all that is holding the wheel to the track. There are times when the wheel gets a molten spot from the friction and gets a bump on it, which can derail the car. At other times, a bearing can burn off the axle or a wheel can fall off. There are derailments that happen because the track itself fails. When cars derail, they often pile up as high as telephone poles.

When the mills in this part of the country began to shut down there was not as much steel to ship. Only the modern mills survived. There was a lack of work on my railroad because it was a steel-mill railroad, so I started work at the General Motors (GM) car factory in Lordstown, Ohio.

Cars are made from start to finish at the GM plant (factory). When I started at the plant, I made car parts. There are several sections in the plant. In one section, parts are stamped out of steel. Another section is the metal assembly section, where the parts are put together to make larger parts like doors and roofs. Recently, the underbody section was assigned to our plant. The underbody is all the under parts of a car. I am the maintenance worker for the underbody section. This is an important job because I make sure the equipment is in good working order for the spot welders who join the parts together.

Today the spot welders are robots. The robots are machines with arms, and they weld the car underbodies together. They do a good job. They do the welding, pick up parts and move them to other places, and hand the welding guns to other robots. If something happens to the machines and the underbody line shuts down, the production stops. If the line is down for more than an hour, the entire plant stops, and everybody is temporarily out of work. When the line shuts down, it is my job to fix it. When I work on the line, I need to make sure it stays shut down until I am finished, so I don't get hurt or even killed. I have a special "lockout tag" that I clip to the switch so no one will start up the line while I am working on it. The photograph on page 35 is of my lockout tag.

My job is very challenging. It's a creative job in which I get to solve problems. The underbody line is all operated by computer. I have to know how to go into the computer terminal when there are problems and see why and where the underbody stopped. It might be that a robot has dropped a part, or there could be a more complicated problem. That is why I went to college and spent a four-year apprenticeship on the job—about 7,000 hours on the job here, so I could learn a lot to fix a wide variety of problems.

In the future, the plant could close, but because of my education and training, I could go to many other places to fix machines. I have a friend who went to Disney World to fix their machines, which include the animals you see on the rides. A machine is a machine, no matter where it is. Once you understand how it works, it's easy to fix it.

Exploring a Career Working in a Factory or as a Train Engineer

1. Have pictures of various trains for the children to examine. Each child can make a train car for a class train that can be displayed around the classroom walls. Primary-grade children will enjoy reading Diane Siebert's (1981) *Train Song* before or after they construct their train.

2. Talk with the children about the need to stop at railroad crossings. Jim Aylesworth (1991) wrote a book for younger children called *County Crossing*. It describes a family stopped at a county crossing while a train goes by. Discuss what Bob Haus said about many people being killed each year by trains. Explain that this is much more common than most people realize—that many people are killed every day. Encourage the children to design (in groups or individually) safety posters warning people to stop at railroad crossings. Display the posters in various businesses in your town.

3. Why do factories operate the way they do? Have each child trace around a simple pattern for a flower, stem, and leaves. Then involve them in cutting out and gluing the flower pieces together. Time how long it takes to finish the project. Then have the children form an assembly line. Assign them to different jobs. For example, depending on how many children are participating, assign several to trace the pattern and then hand it to the next children; the next few children can cut out the flowers, leaves, and stems, and then hand it to the next children. The next group can glue the parts together. Talk with the children about the advantages and disadvantages that they experienced while constructing flowers on the assembly line. Did they feel pressured to hurry? Did they like having only one job to do, or was that boring? What happened when one group was finished and another group was not? What was the quality of the product (in this case, the flower) in comparison to when they each made their own?

4. What is a "mill town?" Explain to the children that a mill town is one that is built where it is because of the mills in the area. Intermediate-grade children will be fascinated with *The Mill Girls,* by Bernice Selden (1983), which tells the story of three girls who work in the mills in New England at the beginning of the Industrial Revolution. *Lowell: The Story of an Industrial City* is a book produced by the National Park Service (1992) that tells about Lowell, Massachusetts, which was America's first large industrial city.

5. There are many different types of factories where people work. Following is an illustration of a shipbuilding factory in Bath, Maine, which is the largest such factory in the United States. High cranes are used to mount the masts and other parts. With the children, brainstorm a list of all the types of factories they have seen or know about. These could be everything from factories like the ship factory in Maine, to ones that make crayons, to Hershey's chocolate factory in Pennsylvania. As the children talk about products that are made in various factories, speculate with them about how the items are made. For example, chocolate is made with big machines, and clothing items are sewn with sewing machines.

6. Involve the children in discussing how a small town can become a boom town when its economics change because a new large business moves into town, mines become steadily operated, or a factory expands. The more jobs there are, the more the community usually grows. Give each child a large sheet of drawing paper and have him or her fold it in half and then open it so that it lies flat. Have the children write "rural community" at the top of one side and "city" at the top of the other half. Talk with them about how a rural community is different from a city. With the children, web each type of community. What is located in a rural community? What is located in a city? See the following example of a city, or an urban, web made by a third-grade child.

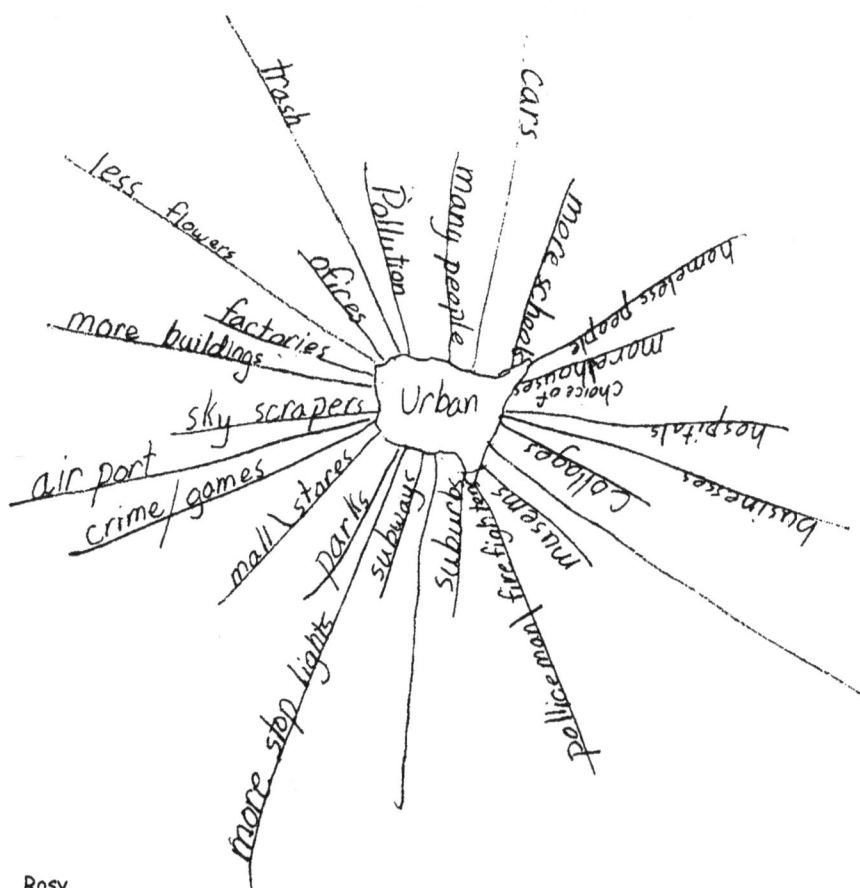

Rosy

After the webs are completed, the children can illustrate a rural community on one side of the paper and a city, or urban community, on the other, using pencils or crayons. Give them an opportunity to share their drawings.

7. Ask the children whether their town is a mill town or a farming, university, or ranching community. Discuss what happens to a community when a major business or factory shuts down. Some children may want to share stories of when their mother or father was put out of work due to the closing of a business.

Bob explains how important it is that he has the education that will help him get a job in many places. For example, he could go to Disney World, as one of his friends did, to work on the mechanical rides. The following illustration is of a scene that tourists see as they travel by boat through the "Pirates of the Caribbean" ride at Disney World. The pirates and animals move, roll their eyes, and talk and sing.

8. Bob talks about the robots that weld the bottoms of cars together. Challenge the children to build a robot that walks or does a simple task. Steven Lindblom (1985) offers some good ideas in *How to Build a Robot.*

Chapter 11

Carpenter

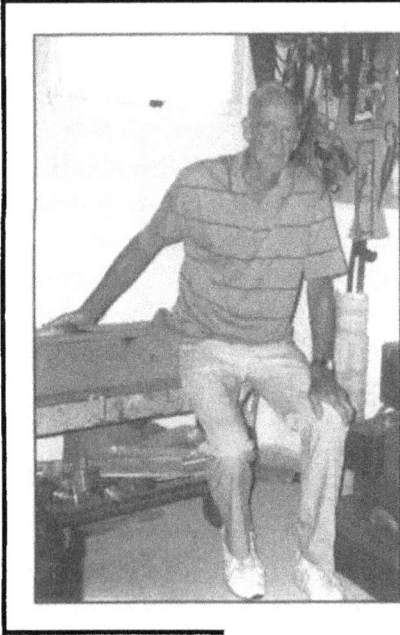

Interview With Keith Thompson

All of my life I have been a carpenter. It has always given me a sense of satisfaction to create something nice out of wood. I started my life as a carpenter by working with a master cabinetmaker from Austria. After I learned many things from him, I left that job and worked with a construction company for three years, building houses. The job was interesting, but there were times during the year when the company did not have work for all of us because of the weather, and at other times they were not building. I decided to take a job in a department store because I had a family, and I wanted the constancy of a year-round job.

At the department store, I did a lot of wall changes. We would change the walls for displays and fix walls where they would hang clothing. The strategy was to get people to shop and see the merchandise. During the holidays, we set up displays on the floor and in the windows. For Christmas we had tremendous displays where animated animals filled four huge windows. There were clothing and toys around the animals. The displays were fun because I got to add my own ideas to the displays and then build the platforms and put the displays together. We also built stages for style shows and wedding shows.

I learned how to be a carpenter by going to an apprenticeship program, and the rest I learned on the job. An apprenticeship program is good because you learn how to work safely and with common sense. From the beginning, when I first started becoming a carpenter, I enjoyed my job. I met a lot of nice people and got to know a lot of people I might not have gotten to know otherwise.

You can start working with wood, too. You can make toys from pieces of wood you might have at home. (See simple toy and wagon patterns later in this chapter.)

Exploring a Career as a Carpenter

1. Have various pieces of wood and bark for the children to examine. Include pieces of wood and bark from cherry, oak, maple, or pine trees. These can be found outdoors or purchased from a lumber store. Involve the children in carefully observing each piece of wood. What do they observe about the wood's texture, color, and odor? Are there

similarities among the pieces? Differences? What about odors? Different woods have very distinct odors. The children can smell the wood and compare and contrast the different odors. If the children get the wood wet, often the odor will be stronger.

2. Involve the children in sanding a piece of wood. Explain to them that the growth lines in the wood are its "grain." Have varying pieces of coarse to fine sandpaper available for them to work with. Let them explore sanding wood. Does the wood look different if you sand with the grain or across the grain? What differences do you see if you use coarse or fine sandpaper?

3. Have the children hammer large tacks into an old stump or block of wood. (Remind them to be careful using hammers and nails.) Have stumps or blocks of different types of wood so they can experiment with hammering tacks into both hard and soft woods. All coniferous trees (trees with needles) are "softwoods." Most deciduous trees (trees with leaves) are "hardwoods." Explain that hardwoods are good for things that need a hard, durable surface, like a kitchen cutting board. Softwoods are used for projects like puppets and pencils, which don't require a hard surface.

   Also, show children some tools carpenters use other than hammers. Talk with them about what the tools are used for and how to use them safely.

4. Talk with the children about how carpenters use wood in a wide variety of ways. Brainstorm with them about the various ways in which wood is used. This could include making houses, boats, puppets, and wagons. Have a variety of woodworking tools for them to examine. Explain what the tools are, what they are used for, and some safety precautions for each. Gail Gibbons's (1990) *How a House Is Built* helps primary-grade children gain a better understanding of how carpenters work with wood and tools when building a house.

5. Ask the children to recall exhibits they have seen in various stores. Challenge them to design a store exhibit and have them illustrate their designs on paper using paints and crayons. They should explain their designs, describing what it is about their exhibits or displays that would encourage people to come into the store or buy merchandise.

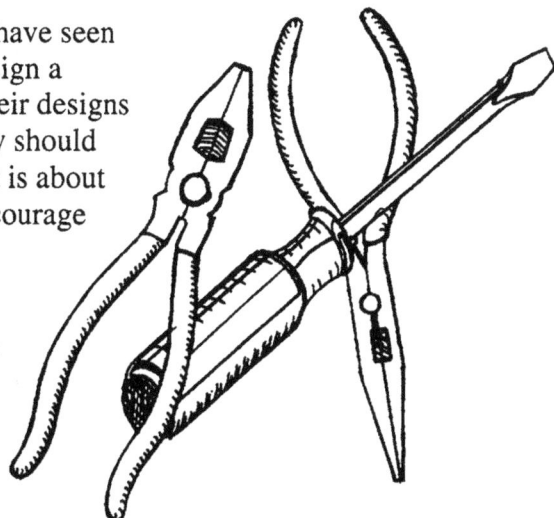

6. Older children, with help, can construct a simple wood wagon using the following pattern.

Bottom View of
Front Axle

Top View of
Front Axle

Rear view

Washers

Carriage Bolt

Dowel Rod

Front view

12"

24"

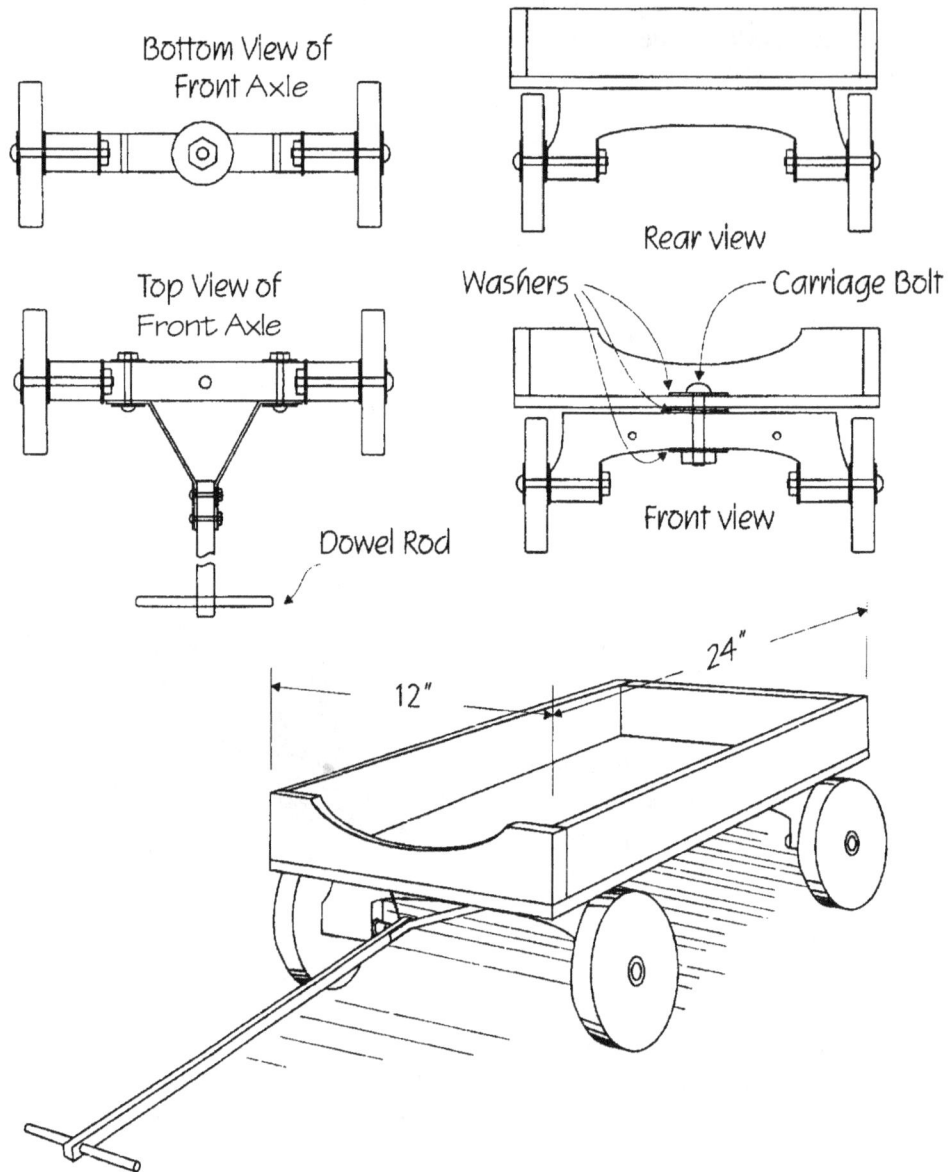

7.   For a wood project all children can easily create, see the following stump doll pattern.
Directions for making are on page 89.

Chapter 12

Child-Care Director for YMCA

Interview With Felix Andrés Arana

I grew up in Lima, Peru. From the time I was very young, I was fascinated by the possibility of working with people and learning new things from them. I learned this love of people from my parents and my grandparents. As a boy, I loved to go to the YMCA. My teachers were interesting and kind. I learned a lot from them, and I decided that when I grew up, I would be like them and work for the YMCA.

When I was 12 years old and volunteering at the YMCA, I was asked to travel to Brazil to represent the Peruvian YMCA. I told my parents that I was selected, and the YMCA gave me a scholarship for the trip.

When I was old enough to work for money, I worked every summer for the YMCA. I would travel to countries next to Peru: Chile, Bolivia, and Ecuador. I liked to travel, and I helped people in many places.

In South America, the YMCA helps people in many different ways than it does in the United States. For example, I had a job with the YMCA in Colombia following a huge mudslide that destroyed a town called Armero after a volcano erupted. More than 27,000 people were killed, and the 5,000 survivors had no homes. I helped them find places to stay, clothes to wear, and food to eat. I also tried to help them feel better after losing their families and friends.

In Peru, the YMCA helps many people who have trouble. For example, they help children who live on the streets. The children can come to the YMCA on Saturdays and Sundays for health care, medicine, and emotional support. During the summer, the YMCA offers a free camp at the beach, which these children and their families can attend. Also, at one time there was a program in which the YMCA started a cheese factory in the Andes, which helped many people have jobs and made cheese available to many families.

Through my life's work with the YMCA, I have done many jobs besides helping people in disasters. I used to be a clown for children at the YMCA, and it was very enjoyable seeing children laugh. I have also been a childcare director for the YMCA. It was wonderful to work with children and listen to their laughter, as well as see the effort that they put into learning and discovering the things they encountered every day.

Eight years ago I moved to the United States. For the past six years, I have been teaching Spanish lessons at an elementary school. Knowing two languages helps you learn more about other people and their cultures. It opens windows to other worlds.

When children become adults, I hope that they remember what it was like to be children and do not forget how enjoyable it was to play. I learned to be who I am by remembering being a child; observing; learning from my grandparents, parents, and teachers; and taking a little bit of each person that I saw working positively with children.

I love to read, and I have learned games and skills from reading many books about children and what they like to do. But the best school I had for working with children was the one I found in the people and children in each corner of the world with whom I have shared my life.

Exploring a Career Working With Children

1. Help the children locate South America on a map. Where are Peru, Chile, Bolivia, and Ecuador? Have books available that contain pictures of these countries and the people who live there. Discuss the cultures and the ways in which children are the same everywhere. Andrés helped families in Peru following major mudslides from a volcano. Explain to the children that the mudslides were a result of the heat and lava from the volcano melting the snow that covered it.

2. Provide children with the opportunity to discuss natural disasters they may have experienced. What kinds of natural disasters are there? Many U.S. agencies help people who have been in disasters. The Red Cross, the Salvation Army, and even the U.S. president help families and communities in need. Encourage the children to find news on current national natural disasters and to bring in news items. Adopt a cause as a class project and collect clothing, food, or money to help families in need, then send the collection to the Salvation Army, Red Cross, or another agency in another city or state.

3. Andrés tells of helping children who live on the streets. Explain that in some countries, and even in the United States, there are many children who do not have homes and who live on the streets. This may be a sensitive issue, because there may be children in your group who are also homeless but live in a shelter. Where do homeless people go in your town or city? Talk with the children about homeless shelters. Brainstorm with your class about projects you can do together to help families that are homeless in your town, in another state, or even in another part of the world. In addition to collecting and sending items, some children may want to prepare a meal or make books and take them to a homeless shelter.

4. Andrés talks about being a clown. Children will enjoy exploring the changes makeup can bring about. With face makeup, lead the children in creating clown faces of their own. Andrés has a great face in the picture at the beginning of the chapter. *Clowns*, by Harriet Sobol (1982), tells children about clowns, their painted faces, and their activities. Before the children begin applying the makeup, have them create a colored picture on a sheet of paper of how they want their makeup to look. They can draw a circle and then color in "face areas" where they will apply different colored makeup. How will their faces look if they want to create a happy expression or a sad, worried, nervous, or scared face? Encourage them to draw several small circles and try different expressions so they can get the look they want.

5. As a childcare worker and director, Andrés is in charge of planning healthful snacks for children, as well as creative games and activities. Involve the children in planning a healthful snack and serving it in a preschool or childcare program, or even an after-school program that they attend. The snack might be cheese and crackers, or they may want to try "Ants on a Log," made by spreading peanut butter on celery sticks and then placing raisin "ants" on top of the peanut butter. Also, encourage them to think of a finger play or a game that they would like to teach the children, or even a simple art project like creating a collage.

6. A talent that Andrés brings to every classroom is his understanding of English and Spanish. Teach the children some common Spanish words that he teaches in his classroom:

niños	children
escuela	school
nombre	name
perro	dog
gato	cat
tienda	store
casa	house
familia	family
padre	father
madre	mother
hermanas	sisters
hermanos	brothers
amigos	friends

Chapter 13

Children's Book Author

Interview With Beth Wilkinson

Writing is a solitary job. Most people who write do so as a hobby. It certainly is not a big-time paying job unless you are super talented like E. B. White or Beverly Cleary. I write as a contribution to society, as sort of a payback to youth. The only disadvantage to writing is the time element. There's never enough of it. It hurts when you take days, even weeks or months (try years), to write a story and your work is rejected. However, a person gets used to that. Honestly, I could paper the Sistine Chapel with the rejections I've received over the years. Rejections used to make me cry, but now I think, "Oh, pooh." Of course, that's the key; don't get discouraged.

Mostly, I write books and articles on social issues and handicrafts for young people. The books I have written include one about making paper and another about tattoos and body piercing. I have really enjoyed all my book projects. Writing is fun. It's a lovely feeling to see your words and thoughts written on paper or on the computer screen. When I was 13, I wrote a story and read it to my class. As I read, my classmates were absolutely silent, and they clapped at the end. It was a wonderful feeling. I felt special.

I learned how to write by reading a lot, being observant, believing in myself, and sending out my stories again and again. The best way a person learns to write is to . . . write. It's also important to read different authors; learn to spell; learn to use the dictionary, thesaurus, and encyclopedia; and take classes in writing and English. Many authors join a reading club and go to a writing group. They also make the public library a second home. Librarians are wonderful at guiding a patron to important facts and material. When you write, make your stories "sing" by using forceful words and cutting out the adjectives. Rewrite, rewrite, and remember, when in doubt, throw it out.

Exploring a Career as a Writer

1. Look at books that Beth Wilkinson has written. Talk about what she would have to do to write her books. For example, for the book on making paper *Papermaking for Kids: Simple Steps to Handcrafted Paper* (Wilkinson, 1997), she needed to research making paper, try several methods for herself, and talk to several people about their experiences with making paper. When she was writing her book about tattoos and piercing, she needed to interview many people for her book and extensively research different tattoo symbols. Books by Beth to share include her most recent one, *Coping with the Dangers of Tattooing, Body Piercing, and Branding* (Wilkinson, 1998).

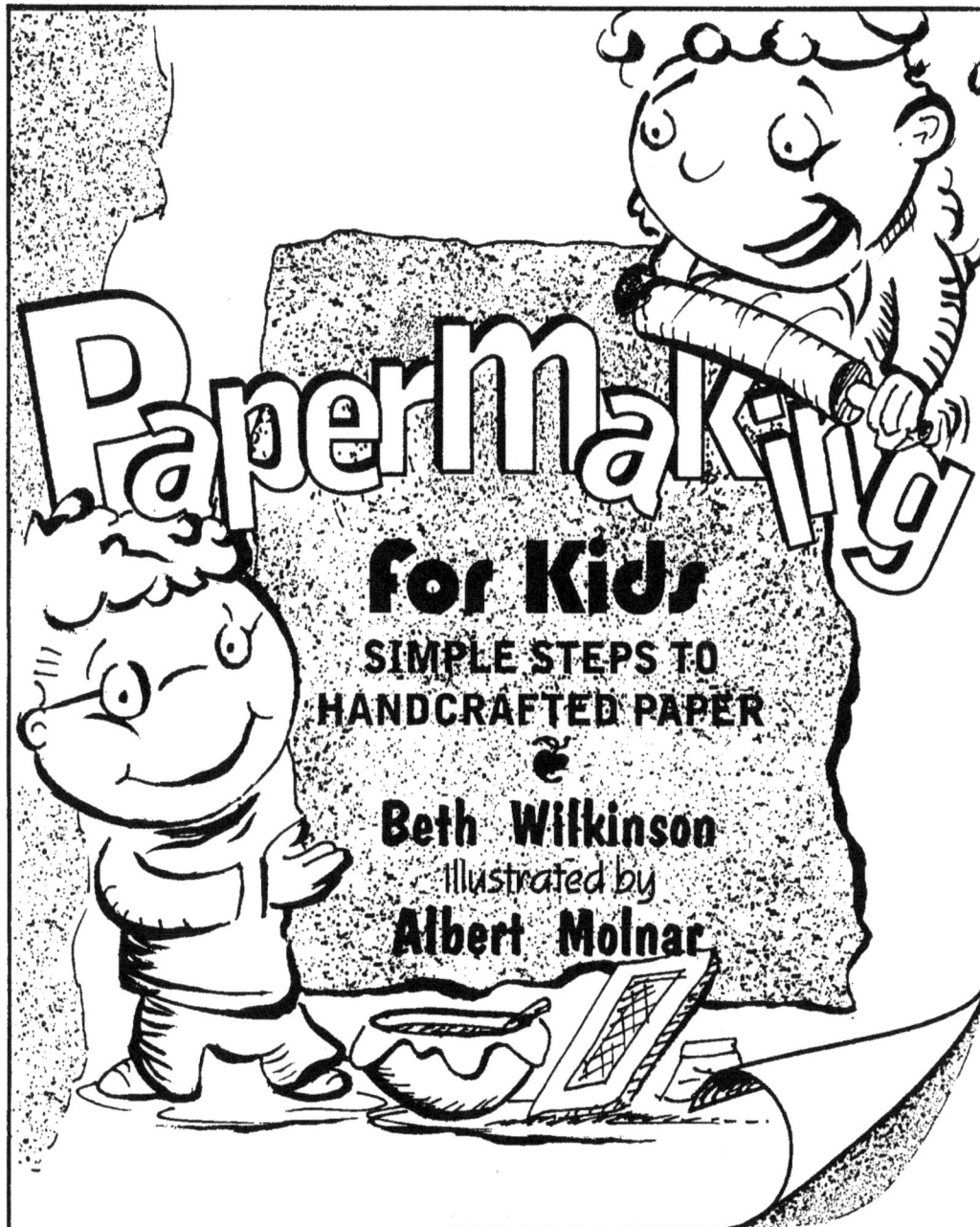

2. Encourage children to keep a journal of topics to write about. These may include interesting things that happen to them, things they are good at and could share with other people, and topics they find interesting and would like to learn more about. Younger children can record their ideas with pictures and symbolic print. Ideas can be selected from their journals and developed into stories appropriate in format and length for their developmental levels.

3. Involve children in interviewing someone about something they would like to learn about. Explain that many authors interview many people as they are writing a book. Have them prepare a list of questions they would like to ask, and tell them to be prepared to ask other questions as things come up in the conversation. Talk with them about not asking questions that are too personal, such as the person's age. A child may want to tape record the responses and then write them down later. After the interview, talk with the children about their experiences with conducting oral interviews. Each child can then write a paper about what he or she learned or work the new information into an article or story.

4. Not only is the writing process time-consuming, but the process of actually publishing a book is also long. A good book for children that explains this process from beginning to end is *The Puzzle of Books,* by Michael Kehoe (1982). Invite an author to come and talk with the children about the process, beginning with having an idea and going on to writing a book and how the book is actually published and marketed. It's helpful for children to hear how beneficial and necessary it is to proofread, edit, and receive feedback on what they write. Authors need other people's ideas to make the book the best that it can be.

5. Involve children in writing a book and illustrating it with a technique like finger-painting, collage, or watercolor. They might even try using a straw to blow paint around on a sheet of paper, making interesting shapes such as a "haggy" tree or monster shape. It's helpful for them to look at books in which illustrators have used various illustration techniques.

6. Some authors write a book, then the publishing house will ask an illustrator to depict what the author has written. Explain that sometimes an author may never see the illustrations until the published book arrives, and that he or she may be very surprised to see how the characters have been illustrated. Invite children to team together as author and illustrator. It is a good experience for the children to think together about how an author and illustrator can best portray the story to an audience.

7. Have children submit writings for publication in magazines, which will help them experience the submission process for themselves and could start them on the publishing path. A good resource for information about magazine and book markets is *Writer's Market* (Writer's Digest Books, 1998). Or, children may find a magazine that they really enjoy, and they can write to the editor in care of that magazine, inquiring about possibilities for publication.

8. When a child writes about a person, he or she should cut out a magazine picture that looks like that person. Looking at this visual image will help with the character development. Also, as children work, they will need some extra guidance on skills involved in writing. Older children will find Sue Young's (1997) *Writing with Style* a helpful guide.

Chapter 14

Computer Expert

Interview With Bill Conklin

On my job, I use the telephone to talk to people all around the world, helping them to solve computer problems. I'm on my personal computer all day long to look up solutions in a database and follow along with the people on my computer so I can better help them with their problems.

I worked for 10 years drawing on a computer for engineers and architects and decided I liked working on a computer. Then I decided I would like to solve problems people have with their computers. The thing I like best about my work is the good feeling I get when I think I have really solved someone's computer problems.

There are some disadvantages to my job. I don't get to exercise when I'm at work, so I make sure I walk a lot when I'm off the job. There is also the pressure of constantly solving people's problems as fast as I can. It's not easy to solve problems quickly all day long.

I get a lot of interesting phone calls when I am at work. Sometimes people do some really odd things. For example, one time someone called in and said he noticed the round computer disk (CD) he had in his hand would not fit into the slot in the computer, so he cut off the edges so it was square and forced it into the slot. Then he wondered why it wouldn't work!

To do well at this job, it helps to have some general background in computers. Then you can learn the details of the work by taking additional courses when you are hired. It's important to continue learning all that you can so you are prepared to handle a wide variety of problems.

Exploring a Career as a Computer Expert

1. What kind of a tool is a computer? Talk with the children about all the different ways people use computers. Some children will be familiar with research, others with games, and some will know how to talk with other people in different parts of the world. Demonstrate different uses, including these and others, and talk about the appropriateness of each.

2. Who in your school is a computer expert? Older children may want to volunteer to be computer experts for younger children, or there may be younger children who can be computer experts themselves. Develop a resource group in your school that can help other students, and help schedule available times for the tutors to work with children who have questions.

3. Most children will not have a sense of what life was like before there were computers. Each child can talk with an older friend or relative and research the use of computers in the world today. Questions might include "Do you use a computer on your job, and if you do, what for?"; "What else do you use your computer for?"; "How did you do that part of your job before you had a computer?"; "Does the computer allow you to work faster, better, etc.?"; and "What was it like before computers?"

4. The need for computer experts will continue to grow. Help the children explore what types of jobs require computer expertise. It's interesting to note how many careers in this book alone require computers. For example, big companies, the space program, banks, and universities all hire computer experts to help individuals and to advance the business or program. Invite a computer expert to talk with the children about where computers are taking us in the future. The children may not be as surprised as many adults are to think about a future driven by computers.

Chapter 15

Creature Effects Technician

Interview With Andy Schoneberg

I am a creature effects technician. This means that I make a lot of things you see in movies. Sometimes the things are scary, as in *Alien Resurrection* or *Starship Troopers,* for which I helped make weird alien creatures, and sometimes the things are funny, like the fat makeups I sculpted for Tim Allen for *The Santa Clause,* or the makeup for Dr. Evil in an Austin Powers movie.

Sometimes my job requires me to go to the movie set to film the things I help make. When I'm on set, I often operate the puppets I've helped to build. That's when I'm a puppeteer. The creatures are sometimes real looking, like a deer puppet I worked on, or the bull in the movie *Michael,* and sometimes they're completely made up, like the Alien Queen in *Alien Resurrection.* When I'm puppeteering, I have to act like an actor does, but I do it through a puppet. Some of the puppets are very expensive, and I do only a part of the movements of the puppet, like the eyes or the mouth. Other people do the other puppet moves. It can take as many as 20 people to work one puppet.

I became a puppeteer on a movie called *Edward Scissorhands.* For the film, I was involved with building mechanical hands for the character of Edward. When I went to work on set with the hands, I needed to be a puppeteer to operate the hands. I have built puppets from the time I was 10 or so, but they were mostly hand puppets made of felt or papier-mâché. I've always enjoyed performing, and it's fun to do either with disguise makeup on or through a puppet. I acted in a lot of plays when I was in high school and college, and even after that, so I was used to performing.

I like many things about my job. I like the traveling that's involved, and it's fun to see my name listed at the end of movies, along with the names of all the other people who worked so hard on the movie. The work is very creative and involves a lot of problem-solving skills. We sometimes have to figure out how to fix a problem in a few minutes, so that the film crew can keep working. That pressure can be very exciting, especially when you are able to fix something that was broken and save the shot.

The hours are pretty bad sometimes, especially on set. On location (out of town), shooting weeks are six days long, and I work as many as 17 hours a day. Being on location, although exciting, isn't easy, because it means being away from my family.

55

I got to "meet" Miss Piggy and Animal once. I was working for the Henson Company, building puppets for a TV show, and Miss Piggy and Animal had been shipped to Los Angeles for an appearance on an awards show. Those of us working in the shop got to have our pictures taken with them.

I learned puppeteering by working with puppets as they were being built in the shops. Early in my career, when there were no other puppeteers on set, I filled in for someone. So, I learned on the job. I think I learned quickly because of my experience performing in other ways.

Exploring a Career as a Creature Effects Technician

1.   Children of all ages enjoy making puppets and putting on puppet plays. Help them make creative puppets to go with a story they know, or have each child create a puppet and then work with other children to write a play based on the different characters they have made. The children can make simple puppets out of old socks or paper bags, then cut faces out of paper or fabric and sew them onto the sock or glue them onto the bag, or draw them on with markers. Stick puppets are also easy to construct. Children can cut a character's shape out of heavy paper and then decorate it using fabrics, paints, and crayons. A popsicle stick or small dowel can be taped on the back to provide a way to hold and work the puppets.

2.   Papier-mâché puppets are also fun to make. For a papier-mâché "glue," help the children mix 3 cups of water with 1 1/2 cups of flour. Cook the mixture over low heat until it thickens to a paste. If it is too thick, add some more water. Cool the mixture before using. To shape a puppet's head, wad newspaper into a ball about the size of a baseball. Wrap several strips of masking tape around the paper ball to hold it together. Another small ball of newspaper can be taped onto the big ball to create a nose, and two more can be taped onto the head if the puppet is to have ears. Insert a stick about the size of a paint stirrer into the newspaper ball and secure it with additional tape. Tear some more newspaper into strips, then soak the strips in the papier-mâché mixture. Squeeze off the extra paste from each strip, then wrap the strips around the ball. Overlap and smooth down the strips as you go.

Let the head dry for several days. When it is dry, it can be decorated with paint, yarn or wool hair, feathers, and fabrics. A body can be made by wrapping fabric or crepe paper around the stick.

3.   Andy tells of puppets that take up to 20 people to operate. Challenge children to create a puppet that takes more than one child to work. It may be as simple as a snake puppet that has a stick on each end (each child holds a stick) or as elaborate as a large papier-mâché animal created over a wire mold that has several working parts.

4.   Andy also talks about times when he has been creative to solve a problem. Involve the children in sharing experiences in which they have been creative in solving a problem

at home or school. One child may share how he or she brings an extra pair of shoes to school to change into after swinging in a muddy play area, and another may tell about a special bed he or she made for a dog that kept wanting to sleep on his or her bed.

5. Many children will be familiar with the Muppets and children's shows that have puppets, such as *Mister Rogers' Neighborhood.* Help them think about how these puppets are made and the personalities that the puppets have. How would they describe characteristics of the different puppets? For example, what is Miss Piggy like? How does her appearance add to her personality?

6. A creature effects technician has to know a lot about acting, makeup, mechanics of puppets, and general puppetry. Brainstorm with the children about age-appropriate movies that have characters or puppets that require a creature effects technician. Children will be excited to think about a career in which they can create these effects. Shaaron Cosner's (1985) *Special Effects in Movies and TV* helps children explore the world of special effects. Encourage them to design creatures or characters on paper that they think would be good in a movie. Older children may want to outline a creative plot to go with their character or even create the character and videotape a scene from their original play using a school or home video camera.

7. *Puppeteer*, by Kathryn Lasky (1985), is an excellent book for children who want to read more about being a puppeteer.

8. When movies are being made, there are many jobs people do to make sure that the movie is successful. Gail Gibbons's (1985) *Lights! Camera! Action!: How a Movie Is Made* is a wonderful book for primary-grade children. Tell the children the following information about Jimmy Archer, a professional props man who has provided props for famous movies such as Bette Midler's *Isn't She Great.*

Jimmy Archer, Props Person

In the illustration on page 57, Jimmy is helping to put up an awning for the directors to sit under while they are filming a scene from Bette Midler's movie. The following picture shows chairs the directors sit in while they are watching the filming of the movie on a monitor.

Jimmy Archer is a props man in New York City. His grandfather and father also worked with props. Jimmy went to school to study business and then started working with props. He organizes the props and sets them up for various scenes in the movie that he's working on.

The picture on page 59 is Jimmy's call sheet from the movie *Isn't She Great*. The call sheet includes information such as which scenes are being shot on which days, the locations of the scenes, the cast, and the props being used. For example, the props for the scenes listed include a briefcase, bags of food, flowers, car plates (1965), car plates (1974), newspapers, magazines, and cups of coffee.

The props person is very important to a movie. The movie would not be successful without the props. Think about a character carrying a briefcase or the 1965 car license plates on a car. What do these props tell the audience?

Involve the children in reading and selecting scenes from books that they like. Have them list all the props they would need for the scene if it were being made as part of a movie. Where could they find these props if they were responsible for them? How will they make sure that the props are authentic for the time period in which the movie takes place?

Call Sheet

"ISN'T SHE GREAT"

Director: Andrew Bergman		DATE: Sunday, August 9, 1998
Producer: Mike Lobell	CREW CALL	
Exec. Producer: Ted Kurdyla		DAY: 57 of 60
UPM: John Mechione	1P @ Location	
First AD: Glen Trotiner	130P Shooting	
Second AD: Dean Garvin		WEATHER: Hazy Warm And Muggy
		High 83 Degrees
		Sunrise: 6:00A
		Sunset: 8:03P

Production Office 119 Leroy Street-New York, NY 10014
Phone: (212)633-9084 Fax: (212)633-1938

SCENE	INT/EXT	SET DESCRIPTION	D/N	CHARACTERS	PGS	LOCATION
42	EXT	HENRY MARCUS OFFICE BUILDING (Debbie comes to work.)	DAY 23 Spring 1965	7	3/8	Location #1 Seagram's Building 375 Park Avenue E 52nd/E 53rd Streets
68A	EXT	HENRY MARCUS OFFICE BUILDING (Jackie arrives at Henry Marcus.)	DAY 32 Spring 1965	1,2	3/8	
COMPANY MOVE						Location #2
140	EXT	ONCE IS NOT ENOUGH THEATER (Her people on line.)	NIGHT 58 Spring 1974		2/8	Radio City Music Hall 1260 Ave. of the Americas (50th Street)
141	EXT	IRVING'S CAR (Peering at the line.)	NIGHT 59 Spring 1974	1,2	1/8	
				TOTAL:	1 1/8	

CAST	CHARACTER	STATUS	PU/RPT	M/H/W	REH	SET	NOTES
Bette Midler	1. Jacqueline Susann	W	1215P p/u	1230P		2P	
Nathan Lane	2. Irving Mansfield	W	1245P p/u	1P		2P	
Amanda Peet	7. Debbie Klausman	WF	1130A Rpt	1130A		1P	

STAND INS/BACKGROUND	SET DRESSING & PROPS	NOTES & SPECIAL EQUIPMENT
		Production: Additional PA's & Walkies
Stand In #1 Report Loc#1 @ 1P	Scene: 42/68A:	Locations: Staging area cars/rigging street
Stand In #2 Report Loc #1 @ 1P	Briefcase, bags of food, flowers,	Locations: Catering Space, Police street closure
Stand In #7 Report Loc #1 @ 1P	Car Plates(1965), Newspapers,	12 Hair stations/EMU stations Location #1
	Magazines, cups of coffee	12 Hair stations/EMU stations Location #2
Scene 47A/68A:		Grip: Crane, 150' Condors2, 100' Condor
2 Elevator Men Rpt @ 11A	Scene 140/141:	Camera: Steadicam
2 Security Guys Rpt @ 11A	Car Plates (1974), Umbrellas	Effects: Rain Towers, Rain
32 Secretaries Rpt @ 1030A	Bullhorn	Dressing: Chang Marquis, Posters, Signs.
4 Cab Drivers Rpt @ 11A		Repairing lines, Pull pedestrian walkway
40 Executives Rpt @ 1030A	Josephine Rpt Location #1 @ 1P	Restaking Chord and Stanrions, 60' Lift
1 Flower Delivery guy Rpt @ 11A		Effects: 150' Condor x3, 170' Condor
Total: 81 Rdy @ 1P	HOLDING AREA	Location #1
	Location #1	Crew Craft Service Rdy @ 12P for #5
	St Bartholomew's Church	B.G. Craft Service Rdy @ 1030A for #81
	109 East 50th Street	Location #2
	(@ Park Avenue)	Crew Dinner Rdy @ 630P for 100
Scene 140/141:		SAG Dinner Rdy @ 630P for 85
2 Ushers (Male, 1974) Rpt @ 5P	Location #2	Non SAG Dinner Rdy @ 630P for 194
2 Cops (Male, 1974) Rpt @ 5P	Radio City Music Hall	Non SAG Crafty Rdy @ 830P for 194
250 Moviegoers Rpt @ 5P/530P/6P	1260 Avenue of the Americas	SAG Crafty Rdy @ 5P for 85
5 Cab Drivers Rpt @ 5P	(@ W. 50th Street)	TRANSPORTATION
20 INO Passerby's Rpt @ 5P		Car p/u A. Belanger @ 1240P then
Total: 279 Rdy @ 830P	VEHICLES	p/u A. Bergman @ 1250P
		Car p/u B. Midler @ 1215P
	Scene 42/68A:	Car p/u N. Lane @ 1245P
	20 Cars (1965) Rpt @ 1230P	
	4 Cabs (1965) Rpt @ 1730P	Car p/u W. Lindenlaub, C.Anderson,T.Klinas @ 1245P
	1 Checker Cab (1965) Rpt @ 1230P	Car p/u L DeVetta @ 1215P
		Car p/u Stills @ 145P
	Scene 140/141:	
	40 Cars (1974) Rpt @ 830P	Director Camper Rpt @ 1230P
	5 Cabs (1974) Rpt @ 830P	Producer Camper Rpt @ 1230P
	Irving Car #3 (1974) Rpt @ 830P	Jackie Camper Rpt @ 1130A Loc #1
		Irving Camper Rpt @ 1130A Loc#1
		Debbie Camper Rpt @ 1030A Loc #1
		Production 4 Banger Rpt @ 9A Loc #1

ADVANCE SCHEDULE

INT/EXT	DESCRIPTION	SCENE	D/N	PGS	CHARACTERS	LOCATION
Wednesday, August 12, 1994						Scribner's
EXT	SCRIBNERS (Jackie with the masters.) Limited Move	134	DAY 58 Summer 1973	2/8		Scribner & Sons Building Berston U.S.A. 597 Fifth Avenue (@ E 48th Street)
EXT	CENTRAL PARK - TREE (Irving's got a new job.)	127	DAY 52 Summer 1966	3 1/8	1,2	Tree: Central Park
EXT	CENTRAL PARK (Hansom Cab Establishing.)	13pt	DUSK 8	1/8	photo Doubles 1,2	East of the Pond Grand Army Plaza

First Assistant Director: Glen Trotiner - Second Assistant Director: Dean Garvin (212)737-7989

Chapter 16

Dancer

Interview With Patricia Conklin

Dancing is euphoric because it takes me to the farthest reaches of my imagination. Dancing is like being in a dream, and when I dance, I can go in my mind wherever I want to go. I'm aware of the audience, but it is a comforting feeling. I want to feel that they are responding to my dancing, and I feel good about that. Most people watching appreciate the dance, and they communicate that to me while I communicate to them through the dance.

When I was three years old, I was at a club with my parents, and I just got up and started dancing because I loved moving to the music. From that time on, I have been a dancer. Dancing feels very natural and comfortable to me, and I love how spontaneous I can be when I dance.

I have danced in the United States, Tokyo, Germany, and Singapore. Japan is where I had the richest cultural experience with my dance because I was able to share dances from the United States with Japanese dancers, and the Japanese dancers shared their dances with me. It was fascinating to see how they related to dance and how important it was to them. I have also taught dance lessons to children and adults in different parts of the world. It's nice to share what I know, but it's not always easy to get the jobs in dance that I would like. In the future, I would like to teach dance to elementary children in the schools because children can learn more about different things if what they are learning is combined with dance. For example, if you are studying about the heart, we could dance out the biology of the heart and its functions.

My greatest love is creative dance. Folk and ethnic dancing, as well as social dancing, are all very pleasurable. You can go to a social dance anywhere in your local community. The important thing is that you are comfortable and confident to get up and dance and that dancing has a positive feeling for you. The steps are secondary and can be learned.

Music is very important in dance. You can choose some type of music and see what kind of movement feels right for that music. Play with different ways you can move your body to the music and don't worry about what other people may think, because it is individual and personal. If you want to start with lessons, creative movement is a good beginning because it helps you see what you can do with your body and with music. Dancing is also about solving problems, and it helps you think about that. After you have spent time exploring with movement and music, you might want to take some lessons to specialize in an area like jazz or tap.

I didn't take lessons until I was older. I acted and danced in the theater before I began lessons. There are still lessons I would like to take to share dancing with other dancers and to learn more. Dancing with others and discussing dance are always refreshing.

Exploring a Career as a Dancer

1. Include children in selecting a piece of music (it can be a song or part of a ballet or other musical score) and moving to the music. How can the children move their bodies so their movement fits with the music? When will their bodies move more quickly or more slowly? What will their arms do?

2. Watch a tape or live performance of a dance, such as the *Nutcracker,* and carefully observe which movements the dancers make to fit the music. How do the costumes help create the impression of the dance?

3. Take a favorite story, such as a fairy tale, and involve the children in planning how to dance it as they act it out. Practice the story dance and perform it for another class at your school.

4. Talk with the children about a subject they are studying, such as the heart information that Patricia mentioned. Problem-solve about how it might be acted and danced out to better illustrate a concept. In math, this could be a story problem or a calculation. For example, 10 take away 5 could easily become 10 children dancing and another dancer approaching and dancing away with 5 children. How many dancers are left?

5. Dance has been appreciated from the beginning of civilization. Talk with the children about the different types of dancing around the world: African dances with masks, Native American dances with beautiful healing costumes, belly dances, folk dances, ballet, modern dance, and so forth. Dances have been performed for religious purposes, healing, wedding and other special occasion celebrations, and entertainment. Many master artists have captured the feelings of dancers. Display prints of paintings of dancers, such as Degas's famous ballerinas and Matisse's modern dancers.

6. Invite a folk dancer to come to class and demonstrate as well as help lead children through various folk dances. Explore the types of costumes dancers from other countries wear and the style of music to which they dance.

7. Good books to share with children about dance include *The Dance of Africa,* by Lee Warren (1972); *Baryshnikov's Nutcracker,* by Norma Klein (1983); and *Dance Me a Story: Twelve Tales from the Classic Ballets,* by Jane Rosenberg (1985). The children will be inspired as they read *Isadora Duncan: Revolutionary Dancer,* by Larry Sandomir (1995).

Chapter 17

Doctor

Interview With Karen Wildman

I am a family physician. That means that I provide medical care for boys and girls and men and women of all ages. I like taking care of my patients. It is interesting to talk to them and to decide what is the best medical care for the problems they have.

My favorite thing is to deliver babies. I always feel like I've done something special when a baby is born. I especially like to show the new baby to his or her older brothers and sisters.

Being a doctor means working a lot of long hours, and I often have to be at the hospital in the middle of the night taking care of patients. It also is a lot of work to become a doctor. When I was a sophomore in college, I knew I wanted to be a doctor. I went to school for many years. First college, then four years of medical school, then three years of residency (where you take care of patients while you're learning). I keep learning how to be a better doctor all the time, by reading books and journals, going to classes, and talking to other doctors.

Exploring a Career as a Doctor

1. Discuss some basic first aid with the children. For example, demonstrate how to clean a cut, apply antiseptic, and bandage it to prevent infection. Talk about what to do to keep a burn dry and how to cover a blister with a bandage to keep it clean. Invite a doctor to talk with the children about other first aid and preventive measures to keep illness away, such as washing their hands, not drinking from the same glass as others, and wearing appropriate clothing in cold weather. Joanna Cole's (1985) *Cuts, Breaks, Bruises, and Burns: How Your Body Heals* helps children investigate different injuries and answers questions commonly asked by children about their bodies.

2. One of Dr. Wildman's favorite things is to deliver babies. Let children share their experiences with new babies in their families. All over the world, people celebrate the births of their new babies. *Welcoming Babies,* by Margy Burns Knight (1994), describes interesting traditions worldwide of how people greet new babies entering the world.

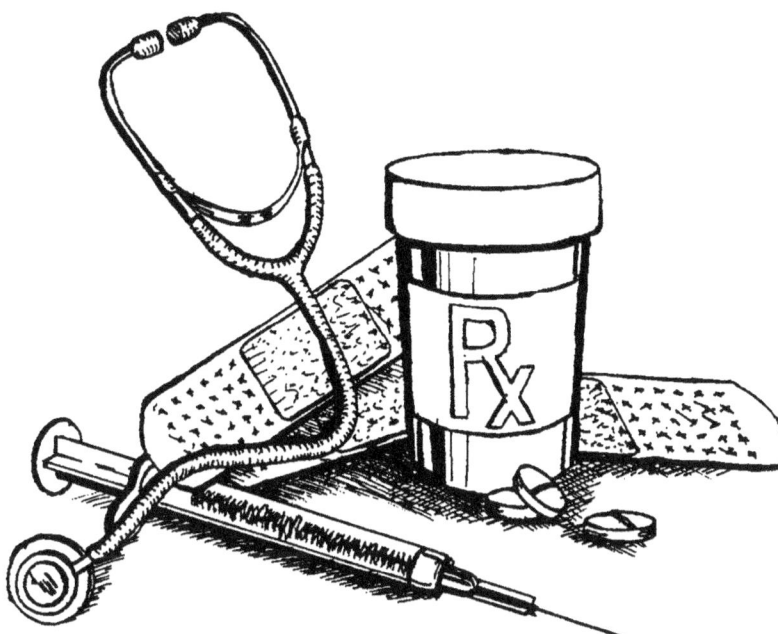

3. There are many more women doctors today than there have been in the past. A good book that tells about the first woman doctor in the United States is Jean Lee Latham's (1975) *Elizabeth Blackwell: Pioneer Woman Doctor.* Explain to the children that today there are men and women doctors and also men and women nurses. A good book for primary-grade children showing how men can be nurses and pursue other occupations traditionally held by women is *My Daddy Is a Nurse,* by Mark Wandro and Joani Blank (1981).

4. Doctors save many people's lives. Sometimes, someone is very sick, and there is nothing that a doctor can do but be kind and compassionate. Talk with children about the many kinds of research doctors are involved in while trying to find new cures and treatments for diseases such as cancer and AIDS. Encourage the children to research famous doctors who have contributed in significant ways to the field of medicine.

5. The children will be interested to learn that mold has been used as medicine for thousands of years. More than 3,000 years ago, people in different areas of the world used mold to cure skin diseases and infected wounds. They did not know why it worked, but it did. Discuss the drug penicillin. Many children have taken penicillin for sore throats and other ailments. Children will be interested to hear how penicillin was discovered. In 1928, Alexander Fleming was working in his laboratory with the window open. A mold spore floated in and landed in a dish of disease germs. When he looked in the dish, he saw some blue-green penicillium mold. All around the mold the germs were dead.

    This was the beginning of the discovery of penicillin. Ask the children whether they have ever seen blue-green penicillium mold such as the mold that often grows on oranges. Since the discovery of penicillin, other drugs have been discovered from mold. These drugs are called antibiotics, which means "against germ life."

6. Children can grow mold on bread from the dust on their fingers, and they will be able to picture the mold spore floating in Fleming's laboratory and landing in the germ dish. To grow mold, lead children through the following experiment.

Growing Mold

Have the children look through a ray of sunlight. They will see lots of tiny specks of dust. They will be surprised to learn that many of those pieces of dust are fungus spores.

Fungi such as mushrooms and molds do not make seeds; they make spores instead. Spores are tiny plants and will start growing if they fall on the perfect piece of food.

Children will be surprised to discover that if they take some of the dust they see in the sunlight and put it on a piece of bread, mold will grow. Involve them in growing mold on a piece of bread. If children use a magnifying glass, they will be able to see tiny threads branching across the surface of the bread.

Each child needs:

a plate
a bowl or plastic bag
water
dust
a magnifying glass

Have the children follow these steps:

- Place a piece of bread on a plate and sprinkle a small amount of water on it. Rub a finger on the floor to pick up dust. Rub the dust on the bread, then cover the bread with a bowl, or put the plate in a plastic bag and twist the top shut. Put the plate or bag with the bread in a warm place.

- Look at the bread each day. Observe how long it takes for the mold to grow. What colors are the spots or mold plants? Will they grow bigger if you keep the bread moist? Have you ever had mold, such as athlete's foot or ringworm, growing on you?

7. Talk with children about how some doctors travel to different parts of the world to help people who need medical care because there is a shortage of doctors. Some doctors go to South America, others to Africa and Asia. They set up makeshift clinics in tents and under trees and see many people every day, giving vaccinations, looking at injuries, and treating other health-related problems.

Chapter 18

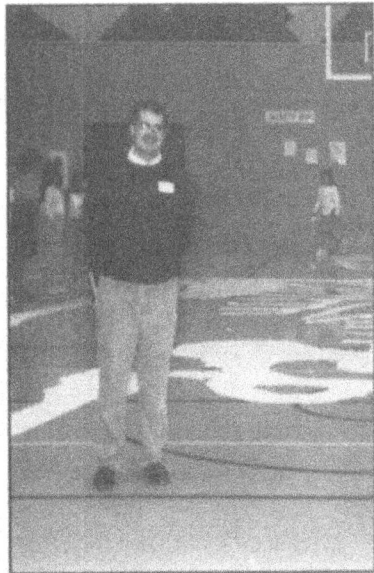

Elementary School Teacher

Interview With Brent Young

My job is important because I am responsible for teaching many things to so many different children. I really enjoy being with children and helping them learn lots of things about science, math, art, reading, and other subjects. The best part of my work is getting to interact with children every day. Each day is different, with new experiences and challenges.

Over the years, I have gotten to know more than a thousand different children through my teaching and coaching, so I guess you could say that I've made over a thousand new friends. Not only have I gotten to know the children in my classes and on my teams, but I have also met many children in other classrooms. I make it a point to know most of the children in the school and go into other classrooms to tell stories and do different activities.

Teachers don't make a lot of money, and sometimes it's hard to support a family on a teacher's salary. You can go on and take more college classes to make more money. The rewards of teaching are great. There are certain things I have to teach, but how I teach them is left up to me. Creativity, dedication, and imagination are left to the teacher, and there are so many interesting things I can do with children. I get to bring in my talents and strengths to help children learn and grow, and it's never boring. Over the years, I have learned some things that work well and others that do not.

It's exciting to design creative lessons that teach children a lot. One of my favorites was having students research human skeletons. We made a skeleton out of a newspaper roll that we got at our newspaper office. The skeleton was made to scale, at a scale of 1/8 inch equals 1 foot. The entire skeleton was 85 feet long! We put it together in the school gymnasium, the only place big enough for the whole skeleton to fit. The photograph at the beginning of the chapter is of me standing with our skeleton. When the other children in the school came to look at the skeleton, my children gave them tours around the different parts. All around the gym we set up booths that examined different parts of a skeleton, and it was like a health fair. For example, at one booth my children told other children that a bone is hollow and has marrow inside.

A favorite activity of my students was when we put a robot kit together, and the robot went down the hall to take the attendance form to the office. They also liked panning for gold. We spray-painted gravel gold and panned it in authentic mining pans.

I learned to teach by going to college and earning an elementary degree in teaching. I have had so many good mentors over the years. This year I received a national award for teaching called the Milken Award. This is a wonderful honor, but the best part of teaching is working with kids. In reality, I just represent lots of teachers everywhere.

Exploring a Career as an Elementary School Teacher

If you are an elementary school teacher, you can involve children in many exciting activities that help them explore what is involved in being an elementary teacher. If you are not an elementary teacher, you may want to involve children in the following activities.

1.   Brainstorm with them about all the duties and activities they have observed their elementary teachers doing. These should include teaching different subjects, talking with children and parents, monitoring the lunchroom line and playground, preparing materials, talking with other teachers, taking roll, grading papers, and putting up bulletin boards. If the children were elementary teachers, which of these aspects of teaching do they think they would most like to do? Why? Which would they least like? Why?

2.   One of Brent's favorite things about teaching is to turn a lesson into a creative learning experience. Have small groups of children select a topic they would like to teach to other children. Encourage them to think about what they would like the other children to learn about the topic and how they could teach the information or concept in a very creative way. Provide them with the opportunity to plan the lesson and present it to another group of children. How can they tell if the other children learned what they were trying to teach? They may want to select a favorite book on the topic about which they are teaching to share with other children.

3.   Challenge them to create the large skeleton that Brent describes, using butcher paper skeleton bones made to scale. Research the body and its jobs and put on a mini-health fair for other children as the children in Brent's class did.

4.   Brent describes a robot that takes the attendance sheet to the office. Children have very inventive spirits and will enjoy designing an invention that helps out with a classroom duty. Steven Lindblom's (1985) *How to Build a Robot* provides information for children wanting to create a robot.

5.   Investigate the history of mining and involve the children in spray-painting pieces of gravel to sift in old pie pans to simulate gold panning.

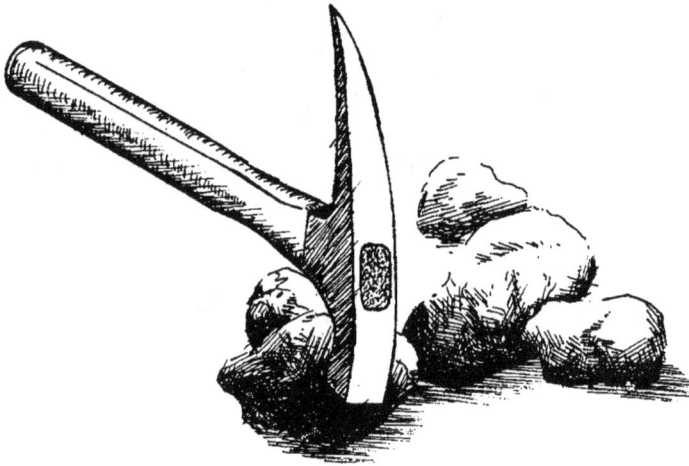

6. Assign different children to be in charge of different bulletin boards in the room. Help them plan what to put on the bulletin boards and how to correlate the displays with topics studied, the seasons, and current events. Can they design a bulletin board that is interactive? How about one that is three-dimensional?

Chapter 19

Fashion Designer

Interview With Jackie Civitarese

When I was in kindergarten, I would listen to fairy tales, and using crayons, I would make different versions of the characters' costumes. Curtains and blankets, wrapped around me, would transform me into Queen Elizabeth. So when I became 10, my mother got me a sewing machine because she knew I would become a fashion designer.

My job allows me to be artistic and creative, and I have a lot of fun at it. I work in a costume shop called The Fools Mansion, in Salem, Massachusetts, designing and sewing outfits that people would have commonly worn in the fifteenth, sixteenth, and seventeenth centuries. Salem is famous for the witch trials of the seventeenth century and for Nathaniel Hawthorne's book *The Scarlet Letter,* so my outfits are appropriate with the historical themes.

It takes a lot of time and interest in history to study books and discover the fashions of different time periods. After I research an era and design a costume, I select fabrics that are also representative of the times and design dresses, blouses, pants, and other items of clothing. The sewing of the costumes also takes a long time. There is a great sense of accomplishment in having been involved in the project from the beginning, when I first conducted the research, to the finished piece of clothing that hangs in the shop. I wish I could have an idea and, "POOF," it would be there, but it doesn't happen like that—it takes long hours and hard work to develop each idea.

Many fashion designers are self-taught through experimenting and watching others work. Others take courses in high school, such as fashion design and pattern drafting, which is what I did. Some designers go to trade schools to learn more and become more specialized.

Fashion designing allows you to do what you want and be who you are. Keep your own style, and all your drawings can be real-life fairy tales.

Exploring a Career as a Fashion Designer

1. Read a common fairy tale to the children. Have them design costumes for the characters on paper, using paints or crayons. They should tell about their designs and why they created the costumes the way they did. They will be surprised to see how many

variations in costumes there are for the same characters. The following illustration shows a troll costume for the troll in *Rumpelstiltskin*.

2. With the children, select a short play that they can design costumes for and put on. Together, create costumes for the characters in the play. These may be as simple as sheets for the capes of queens and feathers glued on hats for ducks and chickens, or they may be more involved such as sequins sewn on black skirts for gypsies or painted boxes with arm holes for computers. Then have them perform the play for others.

3. Lead the children in selecting characters from plays or stories that take place in different time periods. Help them research the periods in which their characters lived. What did the clothing look like? Then have them design costumes for each time period. They can paint or draw the costumes on white paper and attach swatches of fabrics to the sides of the drawings, illustrating what types of fabrics were used for the clothing, such as shown below.

4.   Provide old magazines for the children to browse. What fashions have been popular over the past five years? Have them write a paragraph describing their observations regarding the fashion trends of yesterday. How about today?

5.   Explain to the children that major trends are often started by a creative fashion designer. Have them research the lives of fashion designers they are interested in. What effect have different designers, such as Ralph Lauren and Calvin Klein, had on the clothing industry?

6.   Challenge children to create an original design for an item of clothing. Older children may want to create a dress or pants, or the design could be as simple as painting decorations on a shoe or sewing buttons on a scarf. The fashions could also be designed on paper, using colored pencils or paints.

Chapter 20

Firefighter

Interview With Mark Young

My dad (in the photo with me) was a firefighter, and I was always interested in what he did, so I decided to become a firefighter, too. A firefighter responds to a wide variety of emergency situations. Some examples are fighting structure fires such as fires in apartment buildings and houses, fighting wildland fires like fires in the mountains or prairies, providing emergency medical care to people who are sick or in accidents, and rescuing victims from all types of hazards.

It takes a lot of training to learn how to be a firefighter because there are so many different types of situations in which people need help. When I was first hired, I was trained on a daily basis. I also attended many schools, including The National Fire Academy in Emittsburg, Maryland. A firefighter trains every day of his or her career so that he or she is always prepared to act at a moment's notice.

My job is very interesting and fun because we get to drive and ride on big trucks. We fight fires and save people from harm. We also get to climb very tall ladders, and we slide down ropes to rescue people. We get to talk to children about how to be safe with fire and what to do if they get caught in a burning building. We also have to keep our fire trucks running well and the hoses and other pieces of equipment in top condition. The firehouse is also important and must be maintained.

One disadvantage to my job is that a firefighter works 24-hour shifts and is away from his or her family quite a bit. During these shifts, the firefighter lives at the firehouse. Another disadvantage is that being a firefighter can be very dangerous. During rescues and while putting out fires, a firefighter has to be very careful, but he or she cannot always control what happens. A piece of a burning building may collapse, or there may be an explosion, and there is no way to plan for these things.

Exploring a Career as a Firefighter

1. Discuss the two categories of fires that Mark mentions. Children will be familiar with fires in trailers, houses, and apartment and business buildings. Talk with them about what can cause fires in structures, such as matches, burning cigarettes, faulty wiring, candles, and irons. What can they do to help keep their homes safe from fire? Also, discuss wildland fires. Show them a photograph in a book or magazine of a prairie, jungle, or forest fire. What causes these fires? Talk with them about how some fires are caused

by lightning and careless hunters, hikers, and campers, while others are set on purpose and controlled to thin out the jungle or create a healthy forest. Laurence Pringle (1979) writes about the need for fires in his book for children, *Natural Fire: Its Ecology in Forests.*

2. Share some basic fire safety information with the children so they will know what to do if they are ever trapped in a fire or burned. For example: "Never open a window or door that will feed the fire with oxygen"; "If you are in a smoky area, lie on the floor so you can find more oxygen"; and "If your clothes catch on fire, drop to the ground and roll around to get the fire out." Invite a firefighter to your class to discuss fire safety in a thorough manner.

3. The children can practice calling 911 and reporting an emergency. Have play phones available for them to use, and help them think about how to report an emergency in a clear and informative manner. This drill could save their lives or the lives of others someday.

4. Small emergency kits can be made easily by the children. Have available for each child a small box that closes tightly, such as a metal bandage box or a small plastic container with a lid. Let each child assemble a kit from available materials such as matches, needles, thread, bandages, first aid cream, gauze, tape, and small scissors. Talk with them about the uses of each item and demonstrate how to clean a cut, take out a splinter, and so forth.

5. Have the children read an excellent, informative book on all aspects of a firefighter's job, *Fire Station Number 4: The Daily Life of Firefighters,* by Mary T. Fortney (1998). This book and another informative book, such as *Fighting Fires,* by Susan Kuklin (1993), or a visit from a firefighter, will help children better understand the challenges of fighting fires and the equipment firefighters use.

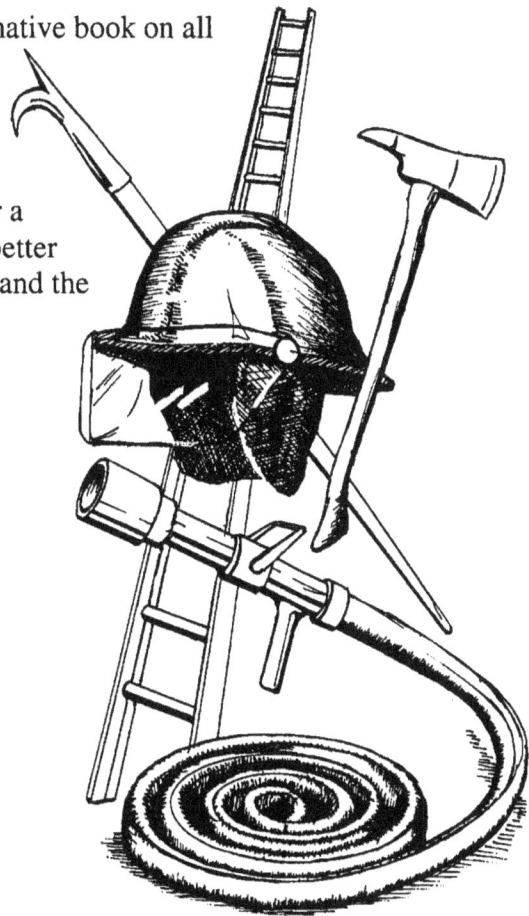

Chapter 21

Folk Artist

Interview With Mamie Deschillie

My name is Mamie Deschillie, and I am a Navajo folk artist. When I was a girl growing up on the Navajo reservation, I used to be responsible for herding the sheep and the goats. Sometimes I would hide behind the hill by my house and make small animals out of mud. Other times I would weave, and once, when I was weaving, the goats and sheep broke down the fence and got into our corn garden. My mother was angry and told me that I had to pay more attention when I was watching the animals.

When I became a woman, I still loved to create art. I would make animals out of mud, bake them in the sun, and decorate them by painting them or covering them with cloth, paper, and other materials such as wool. I started selling my mud toys at a local trading post. One day, I thought of creating cardboard cut-outs. Using cardboard from old cartons, I cut out figures of people and animals. With paint and fabric, I decorated them so that they were bright and colorful. The people I create look like Navajo people, and the animals are everything from zebras to horses.

Now I am a famous folk artist. My artwork is in museums, books, and traveling exhibits. I enjoy being famous, and I enjoy the art that I create. Sometimes people come to my house to talk with me about my art. I speak only Navajo, but my son and daughter help me communicate.

Exploring a Career as a Folk Artist

1. Talk with the children about folk art. Explain that folk art tells a story about the artist who created it, and that folk art reflects generations of people and their cultures. Many folk artists make a living by selling their art. Share examples of folk art with the children and encourage them to bring pieces from home to share. These can include anything from old dolls to weather vanes and pottery.

2. To learn more about Mamie and other Navajo folk artists, read *The People Speak: Navajo Folk Art,* by Chuck Rosenak and Jan Rosenak (1994), and *Navajo Arts and Crafts,* by Nancy N. Schiffer (1991). These books have wonderful color photographs, and the one on folk art contains excellent and interesting oral history interviews. What can children tell about the Navajo culture by looking at the art in this book? What is the traditional dress of the Navajo people? What significance do the children think the horse might have?

3. Involve children in creating a piece of folk art. They may want to try a mud toy or cardboard cut-out like Mamie makes, or they may want to try another type of folk art. A book that presents many different types of folk art and artists is *Folk Art Tells a Story: An Activity Guide,* by Susan Conklin Thompson (1998). After children create a piece of artwork, encourage them to think about what it would be like to make multiple pieces of art for a living. Discuss the advantages, such as being able to be creative for a living, and the disadvantages, which might include having to part with a piece of artwork or the tediousness of creating many pieces of similar artwork for paying customers.

4. Children can investigate folk artists in their community. What type of art do the artists do? Do the artists sell their work? Each child might interview a different artist, and the interviews could be compiled for a resource book about art in their community. D. L. Mabery's (1985) *Tell Me about Yourself: How to Interview Anyone from Your Friends to Famous People* contains helpful information for children conducting their first interviews.

5. Start a bulletin board displaying newspaper articles about folk artists around the nation. For example, on December 26, 1998, the *Denver Post* featured an 87-year-old porcelain painter who lives in Lovington, New Mexico. Cecil Jones paints porcelain plates with scenes from her past (which may remind children of Grandma Moses). She is well known for her windmill paintings, which capture memories she has of windmills her father nailed together when she was a girl. The children will be fascinated by the information about talented and varied folk artists in this country.

6. Talk with the children about the variety of other careers that involve art. For example, in just this book there are Rosy Thompson, mural painter (page 109); Steve Welch, art teacher (page 13); Maximina, weaver (page 151); Zak Pullen, illustrator (page 91); Jackie Civitarese, fashion designer (page 71); and Annette Renner-Richter, architect (page 9).

Chapter 22

Geologist

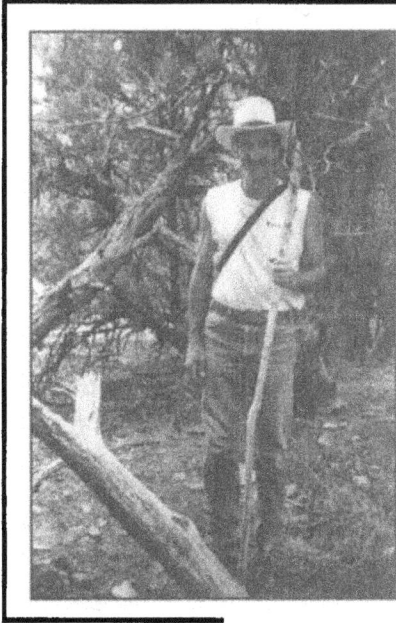

Interview With Esteban Thompson

I am a hydrogeologist, which means that I am a geologist who helps people with water. I explore for and discover groundwater that can be extracted with wells so people can use it for drinking, bathing, and other purposes. I also help people find where the water is contaminated through events such as oil spills or dumping chemicals or garbage into the water or onto the ground. Then I help to clean it up for people to use. A lot of my job involves writing reports about water, so much of my work is done in the office.

When I was in college, I took a beginning geology course and thought it was fascinating. All my life I have liked nature and being outside, and I have always liked water: streams, waterfalls, and lakes. My favorite activities also involve water, and I love to swim, canoe, and kayak.

The best part of my job is helping people. If a family needs water to drink, I can tell them where to drill a well and how deep they need to drill it. If the water is polluted, I can find where the pollution is from and help to clean it up. I have had to travel a lot on my job, when I have to work in the field, and that is difficult because you have to go where the jobs are even if it means leaving your home and family.

Besides water work, I do other types of geology work as well. I help map geologic hazards like landslides so people can avoid building houses, roads, or other structures in places that are dangerous. I also look at places where flooding might occur because you don't want to build your house or a road where a flood could wash it away.

Sometimes, elementary teachers call, and I go to elementary classrooms and teach boys and girls about rocks and fossils. A lot of times, children in the classrooms bring their own fossils to show me. We use clay and create fossil impressions (see page 81).

Overall, probably the most interesting thing geology has done for me is to change my perspective on time. When I was young and in school, a school year would seem like a really long time, and a summer would seem like forever. Or, when you study history in school and learn about the pyramids and how they were built several thousand years ago, that seems like a really long time ago. Now, when I look at geologic features like some of the things the glaciers left behind, even though they are at least 10,000 years old, to a geologist, they seem almost like they were made yesterday, especially when you compare them to dinosaur fossils and other fossils that are tens and hundreds of millions of years old. It changes how you look at time. When I think about living to be a hundred years old, I can see that, in a geologic perspective, that's not really very long at all.

Knowing about geology also changes how I look at the country around me. I think about why it is there. What made that hill? What created the valley? Why is that waterfall there and not somewhere else?

I learned how to be a geologist by going to college and studying, reading books about geography all throughout my life, going to museums, talking to other geologists, and traveling through many parts of the country. It's really important to keep learning new things all the time. That's what keeps me interested in and enjoying my job.

Exploring a Career as a Geologist

1. Involve the children in describing some experience they have had with water. This not only will give them a chance to relate to water in a personal way but also will demonstrate the wide range of ways in which we use water. Involve them in brainstorming about different ways we use water, including everything from washing clothes and drinking to electricity and recreation. Encourage the children to record in a journal the different ways in which they use water during three or four days. Have them share their notes with the group.

2. Explain to the children that about 75 percent of their body is made up of water, and that water covers about 75 percent of the Earth's surface. What happens when the Earth's water is polluted? Discuss how water is crucial to surviving on the Earth. Read the African folktale *Bringing the Rain to Kapiti Plain,* by Verna Aardema (1981). Discuss how we also need water for crops, animals, drinking, and other uses. Explain that a *hydrogeologist* works with groundwater and a *hydrologist* works with surface water. Help them understand that these jobs are very important to the survival of people on this planet.

3. Put a container under a dripping faucet and see how much water is wasted in 5, 10, and 15 minutes. Involve the children in talking about various ways that they can save water. These can be as simple as turning off the water while they are brushing their teeth. Franklyn M. Branley's (1982) *Water for the World* will provide children with interesting information about sources of water, its uses, and pollution.

4. Invite a geologist to bring different maps for the children to examine. What is the difference between a highway map and a topographical map? What does a map key tell us? Involve the children in designing a map of a location. Depending on their developmental

themselves to map the community or constellations in the sky; and older children may want to tackle sea routes, continents, or historical journeys.

5. The children can try drawing an illustration of the Earth's surface from above (an aerial view). What would the Earth's surface look like if they were flying over it in a plane? Can they find pictures in a magazine, such as *National Geographic,* that show different fields and cities from the air? Do things look different if they stand on chairs and look down at the ground? Have them pretend that they are looking down on a city or field and draw a picture of what they see.

6. When Esteban visits classrooms, he shares fossils with children, and the children get to create a fossil impression of their own out of clay. To involve children in creating a similar impression, purchase potter's clay at a local recreation center or order it from a clay store such as Mile Hi Ceramics, Inc. in Denver, Colorado (77 Lipan, Denver, CO 80223-1580. 303-825-4570 or toll free 1-800-456-0163).

To make a fossil impression, press a sea shell, plant, or pine cone into a flat piece of clay while the children observe you. Encourage them to feel and talk about the impression. They will be interested to know that this is the same concept as the forming of genuine fossil impressions. The shells lie in the clay for a very long period until the shells erode away and all that remains is the shell impression. Have the children examine actual stone fossil impressions in a museum or collection or have them look at pictures of impressions such as dinosaur tracks.

Have the children roll out a lump of clay about the size of a small orange, using a rolling pin. When the clay is about as thick as a sugar cookie, have them press an object like a leaf or a shell into the surface or lay the object on a piece of paper on a table and press the clay onto the object. While the children work, ask them which types of textures make the clearest impressions. Cut the fossil impressions into squares and let them dry. After drying, fire them in a kiln.

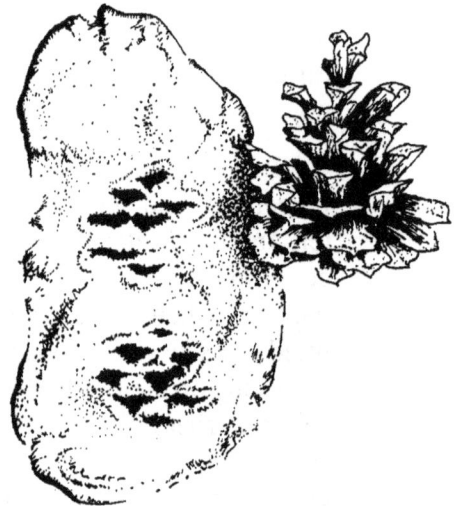

7. A good book on fossils for primary-grade children is *Fossils Tell of Long Ago,* by Aliki (1990). Aliki talks about fossils and has children create a hand print out of clay to become a fossil.

8. Talk with the children about the concept of time. They can create a timeline of their own by starting with their birthdays and drawing in the major events in their lives since they were born. For example, along a line, a child might put his or her birth date, the day Mom brought a new puppy home, the date he or she started school, and so forth. Help the children connect these personal timelines to geologic time as they examine a geologic timeline. Discuss each major historical period with them and help them find answers to questions they may have, such as, "When did the dinosaurs live?" The children will find many answers in Seymour Simon's (1990) *New Questions and Answers about Dinosaurs.*

9. Have children select a geologic feature in or near their community, such as a valley or hill. How was this feature formed? Then direct them to field guides or a geologist who can help them investigate and discover the land features and their geologic history. *How Mountains Are Made,* by Kathleen Weidner Zoehfeld (1995), is an excellent basic book for children that will help them to begin thinking about geology near their homes.

10. Why do so many people build their homes close to the water? What happens when a lake or river overflows its banks? How about next to the ocean? What happens in a hurricane? Encourage the children to investigate these questions. Exactly how close to the water is it safe to build a house? Anne Rockwell's (1994) *The Storm* tells the story of a family that watches a storm from their house on the hill above the sea.

11. For additional information on geologists and what they do, encourage children to read Raymond Wiggers's (1993) *The Amateur Geologist: Explorations and Investigations.*

Chapter 23

Historical Building Window Restorer

Interview With Mark Ledvina

Every window in every building is different, with a different problem when it needs to be fixed. Even if two separate windows have corners that are broken, each one is broken differently. Each problem in every window has a solution, and my job is just a matter of thinking through a solution for the problem. It's the problem solving that I probably like best about restoring windows in historical buildings.

It is very important to preserve historical buildings. Unless something is done to preserve old buildings, such as houses that have been around for a long time, they will not be here for your children to see. There is integrity in helping old things stay pretty and last for the future. A window in a historic building has integrity. Preserving windows is just a tiny phase of a restoration project, but a very important one.

I restore wooden and leaded windows in houses, churches, and other buildings. For instance, I restored the fancy sash (refers to the wooden frame around a window) on Greenfield Public Library, which was designed by the first architect in America, Asher Bedland. Recently I restored the windows in a 200-year-old building, the Rockingham Meeting House, which was built in 1787 (see sketch of building with many windows on page 84). I had to strip paint off the sashes to get rid of lead, straighten the windows, repair them, and then finish them again.

The people I work with are very likable. I also love to go and look at the building with my new windows in it. It's thrilling to me to see that I helped with the restoration. The only risky part of my job is that I have to work with some hazardous materials. For example, I have to be careful when I sand a window that has lead-based paint. Also, the solvents, glues, and other materials that I use are toxic.

I learned how to restore old windows by talking with and watching other people. I started out as a homebuilder. When winter came, there was a slack period, and I had an opportunity to work for a guy who restored old windows. After five years of working with him, I formed my own company. If you ever get a chance to see Rudyard Kipling's house, you can see some of my work because I also did the windows for that historic home.

Exploring a Career as a Window Restorer

1. Ask the children to think about their homes. How many windows are there, and where are they located? Show them many photographs of historic homes, or have them look through house advertisements and realty guides. What shapes do the windows come in, and where are they in the homes? James Cross Giblin's (1988) *Let There Be Light: A Book about Windows* is a wonderful book for intermediate-grade children.

2. Talk with the children about the importance of preserving history and ask them how we, as a society, preserve history. Their answers should include museums, national and state parks, libraries, photographs, relics, and buildings. What do the children have in their families that has been passed down from generation to generation? Have a "preserving history" day on which each child brings in a historical artifact—a book, photograph, doll, or other relic—and shares this piece of history with his or her friends.

3. Many people restore things other than windows, such as antique furniture. It's important in the restoration process that the wooden piece be restored in a manner authentic to how it looked or was built originally. For a group project, teach the children the process of restoration by restoring, together, an old piece of furniture, a picture frame, or another wood item. Begin by researching what the piece originally looked like. To refinish wood, use coarse sandpaper to remove the existing finish. Then finish sanding the piece with finer sandpaper. Finally, apply several coats of a finish such as varnish or polyurethane, according to the directions on the container.

4. Wood items are not the only antiques that are restored. Quilts are also commonly collected and restored. When the quilts are too torn and stained to restore well, crafters often cut the remaining good parts into squares and sew them into pillows, or make stuffed animals and Christmas stockings.

5. Some antiques, or artifacts, are thousands of years old. Restoring artifacts can be detective work. For example, during excavations, archeologists find small pieces of artifacts. They try to fit the small pieces together like a puzzle and figure out what it tells them about the people who lived there. For more information on archeology, see Chapter 1.

Chapter 24

Historical Village Actor

Interview With Evelyn Smith

Genesee Country Village is a living history museum in upstate New York. People come to the museum to gain a better understanding of what life was like in New York in the nineteenth century. There are more than 50 homes, shops, and farm buildings you can stroll through; they are restored and authentically furnished with antiques. There are people making crafts, blacksmiths working with metal, foods cooking, and everywhere you go, people are wearing costumes that would have been worn back then.

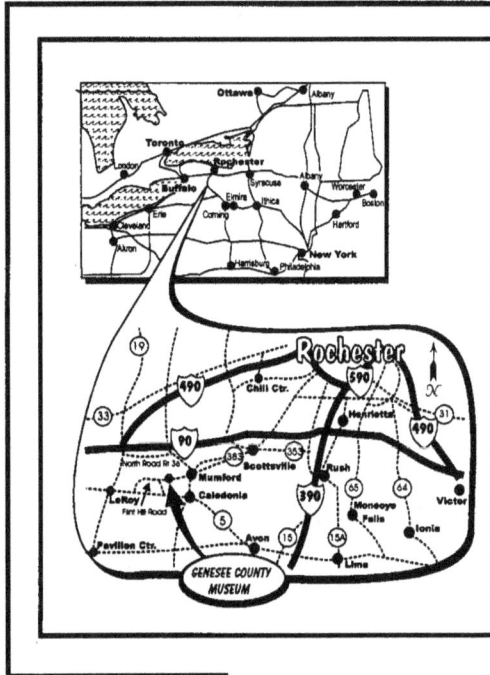

My job is to cook food on the open hearth or in a dutch oven in one of the cabins. As people wander through the cabin, I talk with them about what I am cooking and the job of being a cook and homemaker in the 1800s. Mostly, I describe to people what it was like to be a pioneer and how the pioneers lived. Everyone is very interested in how I cook one-pot meals in a dutch oven, which sits in the coals. After the food is placed in the oven, I put a lid on the pot and then cover the entire pot with coals. The pioneers may have only had one pot to cook in, so they put everything together. One meal I like to make is cornbread and fried potatoes. I also mix onions, beans, and corn in a pot. There is a working farm in our village, and that is where I get the onions, beans, and corn to put into the pot. Sometimes I take the meal home and have it for supper.

I wear a costume called period clothing. The photograph (right) shows my costume, and the boy with me is my grandson, Ben. It's fun to simulate pioneer life by wearing a costume, the people I work with are very nice, and it is interesting to talk to the

people who come into the cabin. The tourists who visit come from all over the world, and the older people tell me about their lives. Some of the things they used to do are similar to what they see at our museum, such as cooking over a fire. We enjoy talking about how things were and how things have changed. On some days, large groups of children and adults come through my cabin—sometimes up to 1,000 people during one day. It can be very tiring talking to that many people in one day. Also, because I simulate the jobs of the pioneer women, I face some of the same hardships they faced. It's very hot in the kitchen by the fire, and at times very smoky. I am on my feet for many hours at a time working, just like the women of the 1800s.

Some of the people who come into the museum are from the city and are fascinated by the way we work. I remember when two teenaged boys from the city were so interested in the dutch oven that they sat for the longest time watching the cornbread cooking, even though they couldn't see anything with the lid on. It's rewarding to provide new opportunities for people. When children in New York are in fourth grade, they study New York state history. This is a common place for them to come on a field trip. Then when they grow up, they bring their children here and show them all the things they remember, and they even recognize me from when they were young. We also offer summer programs in which children get to dress up and play with toys from the 1800s and have lessons in the little red schoolhouse. I enjoy going to the activities in the square, rolling hoops with the children, and playing with them with the toys.

Every year there is an orientation for the people who work here to learn the history of Genesee Country in New York and the history of different houses. It's important that each of us learn the history well so we can answer all the questions and act out the parts in an authentic manner.

Exploring a Career as a Historical Village Actor

1. The children can select historical scenes in books or characters they would like to depict. Encourage them to dress like the characters and simulate the scene for others. What do the characters say in the book? What would the characters say if they were cooking, plowing, and so forth? If tourists came to see the children as they do Evelyn, what would they tell them about the time period and their jobs in the village? Ann McGovern's (1964) *If You Lived in Colonial Times* contains helpful information about the past.

2. Children can create a diorama depicting a scene from long ago. Have them cut away one side of a small box, such as a shoe box, then paint the inside of the box or cover it with construction paper or wallpaper. The children can make people with clothespins, pipe cleaners, or clay and create furniture or other props with small boxes, spools, and other household objects. Encourage them to write about the scenes they create and attach the writings to the backs or sides of the boxes.

3. In Genesee Village, children play with toys from long ago. An interesting book by Bobbie Kalman and David Schimpky (1995) is *Historic Communities: Old-Time Toys,* which shows photographs of the hoops mentioned in the interview, as well as corn husk dolls and other toys. Where else have children seen or read about toys from the past? What toys do they play with today that are the same as those of the pioneers? What toys are the same kind but are now made with different materials? (For example, marbles, formerly made from clay, are now made from glass.) A good book filled with games using marbles is *Marbles: 101 Ways to Play,* by Joanna Cole and Stephanie Calmenson (1998). This book contains traditional games as well as a wide range of new games with clear instructions for young players. Bobbie Kalman (1995) has also written a book entitled *Historic Communities: Games from Long Ago.* Involve children in discussing the games they play today and how the games have evolved or stayed the same. Have them find out which games their older relatives played when they were young.

4. In *The Little House on the Prairie,* Laura Ingalls Wilder (1953) tells about stump dolls, which were one of the early dolls of the North American settlers. A stump doll can be made from any kind of wood and any size of stump. Children can easily make a small stump doll. Have an assortment of stumps (or pieces of branches) available for them to choose from, or go on a nature walk and collect pieces of fallen, dead branches. For the bark to peel off easily, the wood piece needs to be green. The branches can be used as they are or cut into pieces about 6 to 10 inches long. Depending on the age of the children you are working with, you may want to peel off the bark at one end before the children begin this project.

Directions for Stump Doll

Each child needs:

 a tree stump or section of a branch about 6 to 10 inches long
 natural materials for hair, such as corn silk or sheep's wool
 glue
 black paint or marker for face
 optional materials for skirts, ties, and other articles of clothing,
  such as cornhusks and yarn

Have the children:

- Peel the bark away from 2 inches of the upper part of the wood (if you have not already peeled it away).

- Glue the hair to the top of the branch or stump.

- Paint or draw eyes, a nose, a mouth, and any other facial feature desired.

- Add other natural materials for clothing, if they choose. If they choose to use corn-husks, they can tie them off with yarn, or soak them in water until they are flexible, then tear strips to tie around the stumps.

- Describe their dolls' personality characteristics. As the children work, their dolls tend to come "alive."

- Make dolls of other family members by using additional pieces of wood.

Ask the students to consider: Does your stump doll resemble someone you know? Does the doll resemble any book character? How do you feel about making a doll from natural materials? Can you find other ways to make dolls from stumps? What else, besides a doll, could you make with a piece of wood? (For additional wood toys, see page 43.)

5.   In the interview, Evelyn tells of making meals all in one pot. What meals do the children have at home that are made all in one pot? Talk about the advantages to making a one-pot meal such as the pioneers made. With the children, prepare a simple meal such as a crockpot stew. Children can help prepare and cut celery, potatoes, carrots, and onions in small pieces. These can be added to a crockpot with a small roast. Add water and a package of onion soup. Follow the cooking times on the crockpot.

6.   Early American recipes are enjoyed by many today. With the children, try the following recipe or another in *Colonial Fireplace Cooking & Early American Recipes,* by Margaret Taylor Chalmers (1979).

> *Hot Cider Toddy*
> 2/3 cup honey   1 apple
> 1 orange   2 cups orange juice
> 7 cups cider   whole cloves
> 1 tsp grated orange rind

> Mix the honey and one cup of cider well. Add the rest of the cider. Stud the orange and apple with cloves. Add to the cider and heat. Add the rind and the juice and heat a few minutes longer. Serve piping hot (but use caution with children).

7.   In a historical village, as Evelyn explains, there are many people other than cooks who demonstrate skills and trades from long ago. Children will enjoy learning about and trying other crafts and trades from the past, such as dipping candles, drying flowers, and making brooms. These trades are not limited to men. Children will be interested in the books *Butcher, Baker, Cabinetmaker: Photographs of Women at Work,* by Wendy Saul (1978), and *Historic Communities: Home Crafts,* by Bobbie Kalman (1990).

8.   The children will enjoy talking with older adults about how things have changed since they were young. Lead the children in interviewing older adults who have had a variety of experiences. Help them plan questions to ask and talk with the adults. Children can share what they have learned orally or through a poem, story, poster, book, diorama, or report.

Chapter 25

Illustrator

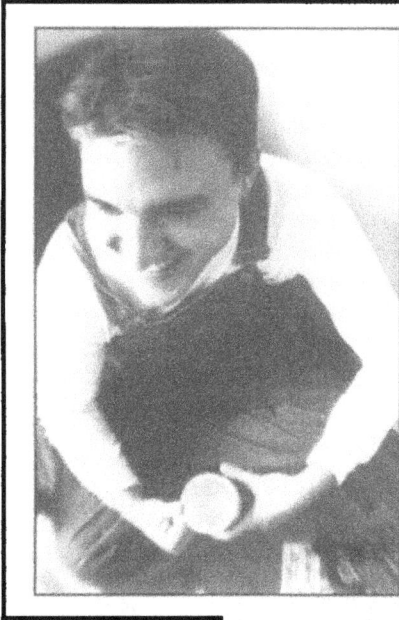

Interview With Zak Pullen

I am a freelance illustrator. I draw and paint pictures that depict or enhance a story, article, or product. Many of my illustrations have been published in newspapers as cartoons. I have an agent in Denver, Colorado, who helps me get various jobs around the nation. When a client needs a specific style, and mine fits, he or she will call my agent, and then the artwork process begins. I create numerous drawings and then fax them to the client. He or she selects one for me to complete. I am normally given about a week to complete the art, and usually have two or three others I am working on at the same time.

I decided I wanted to be an artist early on. I was always drawing on road trips, playing drawing games with my dad, and testing my skills by experimenting and practicing. I decided I wanted to be an illustrator and cartoonist in my first year in college. One of my teachers sat me down and explained what an illustrator was and how my storytelling ability would help me in a career as an illustrator.

My work is the best. I set my own hours. Normally, I work late mornings followed by some very late nights. There are not too many people who can say that they draw for a living. I can. I get to be creative, work with people all over the United States, and do what I love the most, paint.

One of the biggest disadvantages of being an illustrator is the times when I don't have work. Since my job isn't 9:00 to 5:00, I am not guaranteed work every day. Sometimes I go for a week without doing a job for a client. This has its upside as well, though. During these periods, I create work for my artist portfolio.

The most interesting part of doing what I do is how I got here—the friends I met in college, the long hours I spent studying my craft, and definitely the support of the people around me.

I have studied art for as long as I can remember. My formal training started in college. Then I received a scholarship to attend a special design school in Ohio, where I learned from some of the best illustrators in the field. My wife and I will be moving to New York so that I can further my career even more. That is the thing about being an artist; you can never know it all. I am always learning something new. Every time I pick up a paintbrush, every time I look around, and every new adventure I experience, there's always something more I can learn.

Exploring a Career as an Illustrator/Cartoonist

1. What is your favorite cartoon? Have a favorite cartoon day when each child can bring in a comic strip or a drawing of a cartoon character. Create a bulletin board for all the cartoon characters and involve the children in comparing illustrators and their styles. Create a simple graph, charting the selection of characters. How many children selected the *Peanuts* comic strip? How many selected a character such as Miss Piggy or Superman? Why do the children like the characters they selected?

2. Have the children look in a joke book or write their own jokes, but ask them not to include an illustration. After they share their jokes with the group, put all the jokes in a box. Each child should pick a joke out of the box and then challenge himself or herself to illustrate the joke. After they have completed their illustrations, lead them in discussing the process they went through in illustrating a joke that they did not write.

3. Have the children examine the illustrations in this book. The illustrator met with the author to match the illustrations with the writing, but created the illustrations on his own. He went through a process similar to the process described above, in that he had to illustrate material that he did not write. The children will be interested to know that the illustrator in this book is also the art teacher featured on page 13.

4. Children are often involved in writing stories and then creating illustrations for their stories by drawing with pencils or pens. Some books lend themselves to illustration techniques other than drawing. Children who are not very confident at drawing can be successful using other techniques such as collage, finger painting, and printing or blowing paint. Involve them in trying different illustration techniques. Show them books illustrated by famous illustrators who use these techniques, and then encourage them to try the techniques for themselves.

Examples

- **Collage:** Children can examine books illustrated with collages, such as *General Store,* by Rachel Field (1988), a wonderful book in which each item on the store shelves is cut out of paper. Young children will often ask how the pages could be so flat because the cut-outs look so real. Also, Eric Carle creates beautiful collage illustrations that are very childlike, such as those in *Walter the Baker* (Carle, 1972). Encourage children to try an illustration using a collage technique with wallpaper, construction paper, tissue paper, and a variety of textured fabrics. Fantastic sunsets, beaches, skies, and book covers can be created by mixing white glue with about one-quarter part water. Cut colored tissue paper into small squares. Brush the glue mixture onto the surface of the paper. Lay the squares into a design, overlapping the edges so a space is filled in. Paint the glue mixture lightly over the top of the collage.

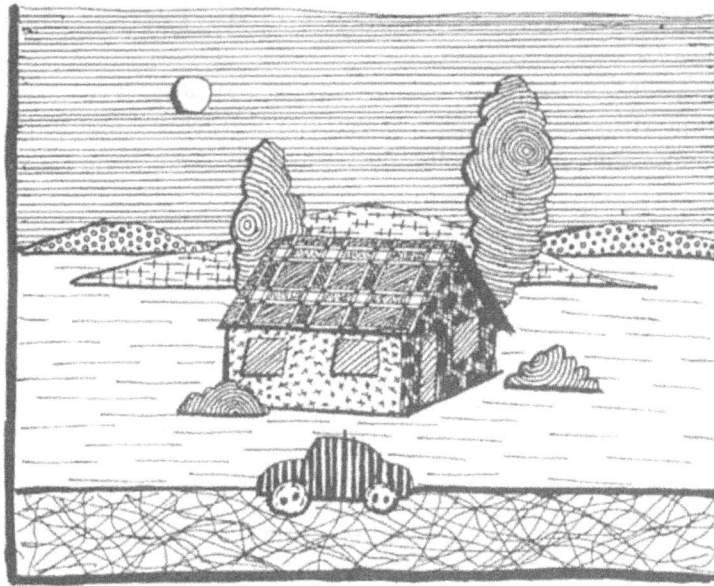

- **Blowing Paint:** Illustrations can be eccentric and exciting. Good examples of exciting and wild illustrations are those by Stephen Gammell in *Monster Mama,* by Liz Rosenberg (1993). Children can explore creating illustrations that run all over the page by blowing paint with a straw. Mix a small amount of water in poster paint. Pour a small amount of the paint onto the center of a page. With the end of a straw close to the paint, blow. The children can control where they are blowing the paint and should work to keep it on the paper. They may want to blow paint and then decide what type of illustration it can become by adding other details using markers and paintbrushes.

5. Illustrations are frequently used with directions. Challenge children to think about something they like to make or do and to write directions for the activity that other children will be able to follow. With each direction, have them include an illustration for each step. For example, a child who is writing directions to create a clay pot will have illustrations of rolling the clay into a ball, pinching the ball into a small bowl, and then adding coils onto the sides of the bowl. After each child has his or her directions written, have him or her trade directions with another child. Can the children with the new directions follow them from the steps and illustrations? Make sure each child who wrote the directions has enough supplies to complete the activity and furnish the other children with supplies. The children will have great fun watching each other follow their written directions.

6. Have several magazine advertisements available for children to examine. Talk with them about the advertisements and how they have been illustrated. Let each child select a product and design an interesting advertisement. Why did the children choose to illustrate the products in the manner that they did? Display the ad illustrations for all the children to see.

7. Political cartoons always have interesting illustrations. Older children will be intrigued as they write and illustrate political cartoons relating to current events of the day. Ahead of time, clip many different political cartoons and talk with the children about what the cartoons are trying to say to the reader. Then have children choose a current event to satirize and develop a cartoon that makes a point for a reader. The class can develop a few newspaper pages of their own containing the political cartoons.

Chapter 26

Librarian

Interview With Glenda Williams

I am a children's librarian at a public library. I help young people of all ages find the perfect book to read. If a young person is doing a school report, I will help him or her find the information he or she needs, whether it is in a book or on a computer program. We do story times for three- to five-year-olds three days a week. During story time, we read stories, do finger plays, and even sing songs with the children. Something I really enjoy is going to different schools and giving book talks and telling stories to the children.

I like working with children no matter what the age, and I love matching a book with a child and having the child come back to the library and enthusiastically tell me all about that wonderful story. I do have to work some evenings and a few weekends.

One of the best things about my job is getting to meet the people who write the books children love to read. The first time I met Jane Yolen (1987), author of *Owl Moon,* I imagined that I wouldn't be able to say a word, but she was so friendly and easy to talk to that it was like talking to an old friend. Will Hobbs, author of *Far North* (1996) and *Howling Hill* (1998), was the same way. He thanked me for helping children find good books to read. I have met many authors, and almost all of them were just the most interesting people you could ever meet.

I worked in media centers and public libraries for many years and liked it so well that I went to college to learn more about being a good librarian. I really like being a children's librarian because I can talk with every child and help them all.

Exploring a Career as a Children's Librarian

If you are a children's librarian, you will be able to help children think about your career through many exciting discussions and activities. If you are not a children's librarian, you may want to involve the children in the following activities.

1. Talk with the children about their favorite books. Involve them in a creative book response. A book response can be a mural, diorama, poster, mask of a book character, play written from a scene in the book, puppet, and so forth. The children can tell about their favorite books and share their book responses with other children and adults.

2. If the children could tell a story to other children, what would they tell? Guide them in finding appropriate stories to tell and help them practice telling the stories in an interesting way. An excellent book about telling stories for a variety of occasions is *Storytelling for the Fun of It: A Handbook for Children* (Dubrovin, 1994). Encourage the children to tell their stories to younger or older children in their school. Sound effects can be added using household objects such as a wooden spoon and a pan. Some libraries record their stories from story time and then make them available by telephone for children of all ages. Children can record their own stories and then listen to them during their listening center times.

3. Teach the children a fun finger play. Children of all ages enjoy traditional and new finger plays. A good book for a wide assortment of finger plays and finger puppets is *Finger Puppets: Easy to Make, Fun to Use,* by Laura Ross (1971).

4. Book talks can motivate children to read a good book. Take a monologue or scene from a book that you would like to bring alive for children. Dress the part (the costume may be as simple as a scarf, hat, or shawl) and memorize the dialogue. Present the book talk to children as if you were the character in the book and stop at an exciting part. You will be surprised at how many children will read the book to see what happens next. After your book talk demonstration, some children will want to give book talks of their own.

5. Involve children in finding out all they can about an author they enjoy. What other books has the author written? What was the author's life like growing up? Why does the author write the types of books he or she writes? Many authors enjoy receiving letters from children and will write back to a child or a class. Encourage children to write letters to their favorite authors; display responses with other information about the authors.

6. A fun library literacy drama center can be set up for primary children. *Check It Out! The Book about Libraries*, by Gail Gibbons (1985), is a good book to include in the drama center. Props can also include envelopes, writing paper with pens and pencils, a date stamp, shelves with books, an old typewriter or computer, and a telephone.

7. Bookmobiles used to travel from place to place so people could check out books. To simulate the traveling of a small library, have a wagon of favorite books that the children select. Everyone will enjoy this traveling library as the children take it into different classes and help other children select and check out books. A very interesting children's book presenting all kinds of libraries, including bookmobiles, is *The Inside-Outside Book of Libraries,* by Roxie Munro and Julie Cummins (1996).

Chapter 27

Lobster Fisherman

Interview With Gary Parsons

I am a lobster fisherman and run a business selling lobsters. I started with 12 traps in 1960, and I knew nothing about the business. It was a hobby for me, and I liked it so much that it became my job. If I had five lobsters in one trap and none in the next trap, I wanted to know why. I would look at the meter and figure out why there were not any lobsters by the next trap, so it really was an on-the-job education. After a while, I had 50 traps, then 100, and then 150. I worked really hard and was able to buy a powerboat. You can start small at anything, the way I did, and make it work if you want to.

Being a lobster fisherman is very hard work. I work seven days a week in all kinds of weather. I enjoy doing it and know that the harder I work, the better my business will be. My business has grown so much that today we ship to buyers who sell the lobsters to restaurants and stores in many different states.

To catch lobsters, I set the traps and leave them for three days. It takes me three days to check all the traps from beginning to end. If there is a storm, the traps may sit for five days. The longer they are in the water, the more lobsters there will be. The traps are baited with pieces of sardines. When I pull the traps out of the water, I have to take the lobsters out quickly. I can handle the lobsters if I don't dilly-dally. If I am slow, I might get bitten.

The largest lobster I have caught was about 15 pounds, but I couldn't keep it. In Maine, you can only keep a lobster legally that measures no more than 5 inches from its eye sockets to where the tail meets the body. Most lobsters caught and sold are about 1 to 4 1/2 pounds.

One of the most interesting things that happened to me when I was lobster fishing occurred when the movie *Jaws* first came out. It's a movie about sharks that attack people. Well, when you fish in pairs, you have a main trap, and at 6 feet of line, you tie on another trap with 60 feet of line. I was bringing in the main trap and working fast. When I started on the second line, a shark went by. I was really surprised, and it took my breath away because it reminded me of the shark in the movie. He must have been 7 feet long and a couple of hundred pounds. Then I saw that he was no longer alive but just looked alive because of the current. The last time I hauled up the trap, he must have been hooked in the rope. I've thought of that shark a lot over the years.

Exploring a Career as a Lobster Fisherman

1. Depending on the part of the country in which children live, some may never have been to the ocean. To build an experiential background, pass around water stones (stones made smooth by the abrasion caused by water and sand), a bucket of sand, and shells. Discuss the textures, smells, and where the natural materials were found. Show pictures of the ocean and beach. If possible, play a tape with sounds of waves washing on shore and seagulls crying. Give children the opportunity to tell about any visits they have made to sandy shores and large lakes or the ocean.

2. Show the children a picture of a lobster. Let them point out how the lobster is measured (from the eye to where the tail attaches to the body). Tell them that a lobster has two claws. One is very strong and is commonly called a "cruncher claw." The other claw is known as a "scissors" claw because it is sharp. Lobsters have eight legs and two antennas. If the lobster is injured and a leg, claw, or antenna is torn off, it will grow another one in its place.

   In a pamphlet that Gary publishes on lobsters, he provides these additional facts:

   • Each female lobster can lay between 5,000 and 160,000 eggs in her lifetime.

   • Lobsters migrate to deeper waters offshore in the winter.

   • Years ago, lobsters were not considered good to eat. They were so plentiful that after a large storm they would often wash up on shore and be collected to be used as fertilizer in island gardens.

   • There are left- and right-handed lobsters; some have their large (crusher) claw on the right, and some have it on the left.

3. Jerry Pallotta and Rob Bolster's (1990) *Going Lobstering* tells the story of lobstering in an interesting way, with beautiful illustrations.

4. Lobster traps are different from many other types of traps. Lobsters can get into the traps but cannot leave them. If possible, borrow a lobster trap or show the children a picture of one in a book and explain how the trap works. They will be interested in seeing the section of the trap that contains the dead fish and the compartment that holds the lobsters and other fish that get caught in the trap until the fisherman can take them out.

5. Fishermen can tell where they put the traps because they mark the traps with a wood or styrofoam buoy, which floats on the surface. Buoys are like cattle brands because each fisherman has a different pattern and color combination, and no two are alike. Some have the same color combination, but the patterns and designs are different, so each fisherman knows exactly which is his or hers. Lead children in cutting a buoy shape out of a piece of white paper. Each child can design his or her buoy differently, and the buoys can be hung around the room using pieces of cord or yarn.

6. Lobster fishermen, like other fishermen, can get lost at sea during a storm. For many years, lighthouses helped fishermen find their way and warned them of coastal dangers. Today many lighthouses operate with electrical lights. *Keep the Lights Burning, Abbie* is a wonderful historical book by Peter Roop and Connie Roop (1985) about a lighthouse in the 1800s and how a girl named Abbie kept the light burning during a storm.

7. Talk with the children about how people cook lobsters. Without the demand for lobster meat, lobster fishermen would not have a business. Bring lobster meat for the children to try. Discuss the taste, smell, and texture of the meat. How would children describe lobster meat and how it tastes?

8. Involve them in creating a beautiful ocean simulation. Hang a sheet from the ceiling to create a screen. Provide the children with books containing pictures of sea life to examine. Using crayons, they can draw sea animals on a stiff piece of paper. Have them cut around the outsides of the sea creatures and, on a separate piece of paper, write poems about their sea animals. Project a light from a lamp or an overhead projector onto the sheet. The children can sit on the other side of the sheet and be the audience. One child at a time can pin or tape his or her sea creature to one side of the sheet (the side the light is projected onto, on the other side from the audience) and read his or her poem. Then the next child can take a turn, and so forth until the sheet becomes an ocean filled with creatures devised by the children. The projected light will give the sheet scene the look of wavering water.

9. Wonderful "sea prints" can be made using discarded (but unused) styrofoam meat trays. The butcher at your local grocery story will usually give away meat trays for school projects. Children can sketch a fish on a styrofoam tray using a pencil. Then they can use the back end of a paintbrush or another thin stick to etch over the pencil drawing, making a fairly deep impression. Using a paintbrush, they can paint over the entire surface of the etching, then carefully lay the tray, paint-side down, on a piece of paper. When they lift the tray straight up (to avoid smearing), the print will be completed and resemble a fish in water.

Chapter 28

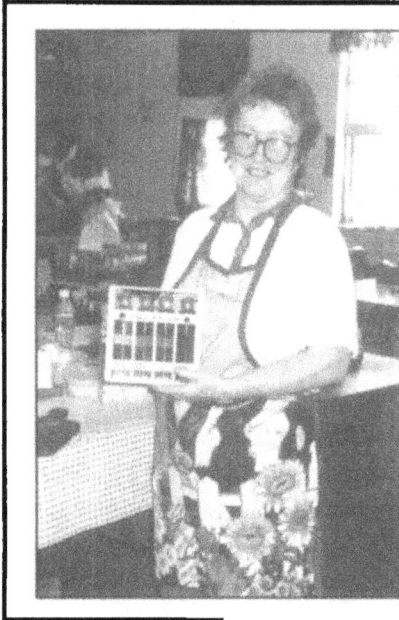

Maple Syrup and Cheese Business Owner

Interview With Betsy Ayers Luce

My husband, Larry, and I age and smoke cheese and sell maple syrup at our farm, Sugarbush Farm, which is located in Woodstock, Vermont. We have another farm where we keep the dairy cows, and I help milk them and help feed the calves. Then I come to Sugarbush, where I manage the production and sales of our products.

At Sugarbush, I am also in charge of taking the orders, hiring the employees, and packing the cheese and syrup for mailing. We sell large quantities of syrup and cheese: In December 1998 we received 1,900 telephone calls for orders. Each year we sell about 3,000 gallons of syrup. We store the syrup in 30-gallon drums to keep it cool. Each week we have to decide which grade of syrup to put into the jugs for shipping, depending on the orders we have received.

I started working at the farm when I was four or five years old. It was our family's business, and my job was to hang a tag with our business name on it on each jug of syrup. Now the jugs have our name on the label. I was pleased, when I was young, to have a job because I had a horse and I needed to earn money for its shoes and grain. My grandchildren work in the family business now when they are not in school. Elizabeth is 12 and runs the cash register. Tim is 10, and he enjoys giving tours to the sugar house and in the woods where we tap the trees. He tells all the tourists about how we make our syrup.

Our business is hard work because we work seven days a week, and the work is never done. Every day the farm animals require care, and we have customers every day because the store is always open. The trees also have to be taken care of on a regular basis. Last year we had a bad ice storm, and we are still cutting down the branches that were damaged during the storm. We have to keep up on our firewood so that we will have enough wood to boil the sap for the syrup.

It bothers me that so many children have no contact with the cows and other animals that give them milk, meat, and eggs. Some children today think that these products simply "come from the store," and it makes me feel glad when we are able to help them understand not only where the products come from, but also the work that goes into bringing them from a farm to their tables. It's every farmer's job to make sure that children know that farmers are important and that

103

there are real people behind all that they eat. Then they will appreciate something like maple syrup and will never look at syrup the same way again.

Below is a story we wrote about how we make our maple syrup and cheese.

The Maple Syrup Making Story

The Tapping

Maple trees grow wild from natural self-seeding. Where large groups of maple trees grow and are used for maple syrup production, the area is called a "Sugarbush." Here on our farm we tap about 3,500 maple trees. A tree must be at least 40 years old to be tapped. We make roads into the forest to the areas where there is the heaviest concentration of sugar maples. Other species of trees are thinned out to allow the maple trees more room to grow and more access to the sunlight and natural nutrients in the ground.

The maple sugar season is about six weeks long and usually starts in late February or early March. When the days begin to get warmer, we start drilling the tap holes. A hole is drilled about two inches deep and a quarter-inch in diameter, usually with a power drill. Many years the snow is several feet deep at this time of year, and we use snowshoes to get around in the woods. Once the hole is drilled and the shavings are brushed out, a metal spout is hammered into the tree. Next, a 16-quart sap bucket is hung and a cover attached to keep out the rain and snow (see illustration). A newer way to collect sap is with plastic tubing. Plastic spouts are driven into the trees, and up to 100 trees are connected together with plastic tubing. The sap runs down the hill in the tubing and is collected in a large tub at the bottom of the hill. This saves a great deal of labor in the collection process.

How and Why Does the Sap Drip from the Tree?

Maple sap is the combination of water that is stored in the tree's roots and natural maple sugar that was produced during the past summer in the tree. On a warm day, the water flows up from the roots, mixes with the natural sugar, and produces sap. Sap is between 2 and 5 percent natural sugar and is thin and clear. Typical sugar weather sees a freeze at night and a thaw the next day. This causes the sap to be pushed out the spout hole. The amount of sap that drips out into one bucket on a given day can vary from none to over 16 quarts, depending on things like temperature during the day, wind, and barometric pressure. A tree can be tapped each year without harm, but a new hole must be drilled six inches from the previous year's hole. The sugaring process takes only 7 percent of the sap, so it's not harmful to the tree.

Sap Collection

Each day the sap drips, it must be collected, because it is perishable until it is boiled. The sugarmaker heads out with a sled or wagon pulled by a team of horses or a tractor. He or she goes to each sap bucket, dumps the sap into a collection pail, and carries it back to the sled, where it is dumped into a gathering tank. A typical sap collection day would find a crew of four people, taking eight hours to collect about 1,200 buckets, trudging many times through snow two or three feet deep. With the plastic pipeline, the sap is pumped from many collection tubs throughout the woods once a day.

The Sugarhouse

A sugarhouse contains the evaporator, which is the large pan and firebox used to boil the sap down into syrup. Sap is brought from the woods and dumped into a storage tank. We need about 1,500 gallons of sap before we have enough to start our fire and begin to boil. The sugarhouse also has an outside wood shed where about 25 to 35 cords of wood have been cut, stacked, and dried for about a year to use as fuel to boil the sap. During the sugar season, a family spends most of their waking hours in the sugarhouse. It becomes the gathering place for neighbors and friends, with many meals served right in the sugarhouse, because the person who does the boiling can't leave the job.

The Boiling Process

The evaporator is divided into two pans, one for the front and one for the back. The sap flows into the back pan by way of a pipe and float box—all the while a certain depth is maintained. The sap enters the pan at between 2 and 4 percent sugar, and enough water boils away so the sap is reduced to liquid that is 7 percent sugar. It then flows into the first compartment of the front pan and continues its way through several sections where it is gets thicker and thicker. So much steam is generated with the boiling away of the water that it is hard to see from one end of the building to the other. Three-foot-long logs are fed into the firebox, and the sugarmaker adds more firewood about every five minutes. The sugarmaker keeps checking the thickness of the syrup to know exactly when it has reached the correct thickness as set by State of Vermont standards. He checks this by using a thermometer (maple syrup is syrup at 219 degrees F) and a hydrometer, which measures the exact density. When the batch is right, the sugar-maker opens the spigot and "draws off" maple syrup, usually about one to three gallons at a time, while more sap continues to flow into the pans. This process is repeated over and over again throughout the sugaring season. At no time during the boiling process can the operator leave the job, because the depth of the sap is only a couple of inches in the boiling pan and inattention could cause the pan to scorch and the syrup to be burned. When "extra good" sap days occur, the boiling can extend far into the night to keep up with the large amounts of sap. The syrup is filtered and stored either in plastic jugs for immediate sale or 30-gallon drums for storage for future canning needs.

Maple Storage and Uses

Maple syrup is hot-packed in cans and jugs and, unopened, will keep for at least two years. Once it has been opened, it must be refrigerated because it contains no preservatives and will begin to ferment if left at room temperature. In the refrigerator, it will keep another year or more. It can also be frozen, but space should be allowed in the container for expansion upon freezing.

Maple syrup is graded according to Vermont Department of Agriculture standards. The grades are based on color and strength of flavor. Syrup made early in the season usually is of the lighter grades, and as the weather gets warmer and the tree gets closer to putting forth its buds, the syrup becomes a darker color and a stronger maple flavor. No one grade is better than any other; it's just one's personal preference. All containers packed in Vermont must have a grade sticker on the container as well as the sugarmaker's name and address. Many sugarmakers use very similar containers, because the industry is so small that only two container companies make the syrup containers. Types of grades are:

Fancy Grade: Very light in color and a delicate, light taste.
Grade A Medium: A bit more maple flavor, slightly darker. A good all-around
                           table syrup.
Grade A Dark: A nice strong maple flavor; excellent for both table and cooking.
Grade B: Made at the end of the season; extra strong and excellent
                           for cooking and those who enjoy the robust taste for table use.

Uses for Maple Syrup

Common uses are for pancakes, waffles, and French toast (the syrup can be heated in a microwave oven for 15 seconds before using). Heat and pour over ice cream. Cooking uses for maple syrup include glazes; barbecue sauce; and sweetening for carrots, winter squash, grapefruit, yogurt, hot cereal, pumpkin pie, or pecan pie. Maple syrup can also be substituted for granulated sugar in cooking. Generally, use 3/4 cup of maple syrup for 1 cup of white sugar and also cut down on the amount of liquid in the recipe.

Exploring a Career With a Home Business:
Maple Syrup and Cheese

1. The children can write to the Luces at Sugarbush Farm, RR1, Box 568, Woodstock, VT 05091. Help them think of questions they would like to ask and comments they would like to make about maple syrup and cheese. The Luces have a story for children about how cheese is made, which they will send upon request (include a self-addressed, stamped envelope with your request).

2. Have maple syrup available for the children to taste. They will enjoy trying it over squash, in yogurt, on hot cereal, or any of the other uses suggested by the Luces. If possible, provide children with several different grades to compare and contrast. If you do not have access to real maple syrup, explain to the children that they can make syrup that has artificial maple flavoring by heating water and sugar together until it boils, then adding a few drops of maple flavoring.

3. The children will be interested in sampling various cheeses. Provide small samples of different varieties and discuss each type as children sample it. Which cheese has the strongest taste and odor? Which cheese is usually used on spaghetti, over salads, and in chili? How about in cheesecake? (For this activity, check first with parents to make sure the children do not have an allergy to milk and milk products.)

4. Grandma Moses, a famous folk painter, created charming paintings that depict people doing ordinary things on their land in Vermont, such as making maple syrup from maple trees. Grandma Moses's painting "Maple Bush," painted in 1953 with oil on masonite, is a wonderful scene of sap being collected from maple trees, created from a memory that she had. The children will be inspired to learn more about this artist who lived in Vermont near where the Luces live. Two fascinating children's books about Grandma Moses's life are *Grandma Moses: Painter of Rural America,* by Zibby Oneal (1986), and *Barefoot in the Grass: The Story of Grandma Moses,* by William H. Armstrong (1970).

5. Talk with the children about how Betsy wants all children to understand where their food comes from. For one day, have each child record everything he or she eats. For packaged foods, the child can inspect the package to find out which ingredients were used. Next to the food item, have him or her indicate where the food came from (for example, next to the recorded item *cookies,* should be "oatmeal from plants," "butter from cows," "eggs from chickens," and "sugar from sugarcane"). With the children, discuss the foods and their original sources.

6. Children will love the beautiful photographs in Kathryn Lasky's (1983) *Sugaring Time,* a Newbery Honor book about sugaring in Vermont.

With the children, read the following section about Richard Bangen, a different type of farmer.

Another Kind of Farmer: Richard Bangen

All my life I wanted to be a farmer. I was born on the farm that I live on now. My father was a farmer, and he taught me how to farm. Being a farmer allows you to have almost complete independence, in that you can do things when you want because you are your own boss. Being a farmer is also a lot of work. You work from early in the morning to late at night, and your work is still not done. Also, you are responsible to make sure that the farm and ranch run smoothly. If you do not work, then the work does not get done because there is no one else to do the jobs.

Ranchers do a lot of different things. They fix fences, bale hay, haul hay, put up hay, haul cattle, sell cattle, buy cows, and buy bulls. General farmers work the ground; seed the wheat, oats, and barley; combine crops; and sell the crops.

Talk with the children about types of farmers other than those who farm maple syrup. Primary-grade children will enjoy Gail Gibbons's (1988) *Farming,* and children of all ages will enjoy the beautiful photographs in *The American Family Farm,* by George Ancona and Joan Anderson (1989), and Nancy Price Graff's (1989) *The Strength of the Hills: A Portrait of a Family Farm.*

Chapter 29

Mural Painter

Interview With Rosalie Thompson

Creating things has always fascinated me. I really enjoy the process of creating art and designing original patterns. Over the years, I have painted and drawn many pictures; made tables and pots from clay; created sculptures with wires, clay, marble, and papier-mâché; colored fabric with tie dyes, silk paints, and ink; made mosaic designs; woven rugs and wall hangings; and taken many photographs in color and black and white. Presently, I am making many quilts and designing costumes for plays.

Last summer, I painted a very large mural on the wall of a YMCA children's center. I had the entire blank wall, and I could do anything I wanted as long as I had the idea approved. It was exciting to think of a design for a wall that small children would like to see every day. The design I painted was one of a jungle with many different brightly colored animals. First, I drew the design on paper and painted it the colors I wanted to use on the wall. Then I went to paint stores and selected the paint. The wall was white, so I painted it light blue to make a better background for the jungle. When the blue paint was dry, I sketched the design on the wall using a pencil, and then I painted the plants and animals. The entire mural took about 100 hours to paint. The children loved it, and it was fun to hear the children talking and asking me questions about how I painted the mural.

I love the process of art. It is exciting to express yourself through the use of different materials. The hard part is when someone wants me to create something in particular and I don't really like his or her idea. Then it is hard for me to create, but I have to create it that way because the client pays me to do the work.

It's nice to see my artwork displayed and know that people are enjoying it. Be creative and express who you are through art. Always be on the lookout for art around you such as murals in libraries and statues on lawns. Other people's art can inspire you and help you become more creative with your own ideas.

Exploring a Career as a Mural Painter

1. Encourage children to explore art in their community. Where are murals, statues, or interestingly designed buildings and other structures located? Challenge children to think about how an area in their community might be enhanced by art. Explain to the children that when we talk about the beauty around us, we refer to this as aesthetics.

2. Throughout history, artists have painted murals to communicate and to make a wall beautiful. Murals can be painted or can be made from mosaics, tiles, and other materials. Encourage children to learn about famous artists, such as Picasso or Diego Rivera, who have painted murals. A good children's book about Diego Rivera is *Diego,* by Jeanette Winter (1991).

3. Involve children in painting a mural as a group or individually. Provide them with a theme such as "equality" or "kindness." Pieces of butcher paper work well, or there may be a blank wall in your building that you would like to have decorated with a mural. If working as a group, encourage each child to think of an idea for the mural and then have the group decide together how to incorporate all the ideas. Or assign a leader to the group, have the group discuss possibilities for the mural, and then the leader can assign roles for the group members such as someone who sketches, another who paints the sky, and so forth.

Chapter 30

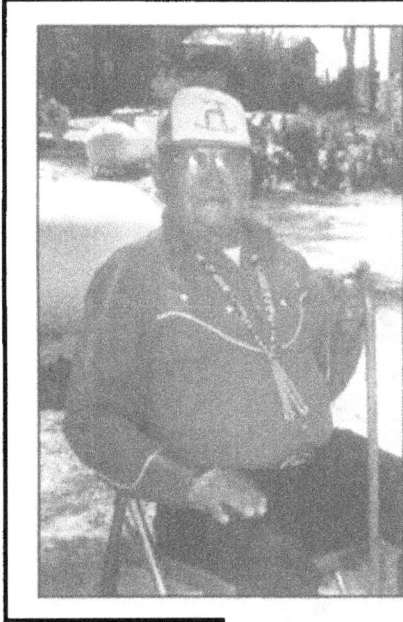

Navajo Medicine Man

Interview With James Joe

I learned to be a medicine man from my grandfather, who was a medicine man. My mother died from the measles when I was five years old. I went to live with my grandfather and grandmother in a hogan in Sheep Springs, New Mexico.

My grandfather taught me how to sing, pray, and help heal people who are sick. He would keep me up all night long listening to what he had to say about the Navajo traditions, ceremonies, and medicine. I would keep the fire going as he talked. He also told me magical stories about coyotes, deer, bears, and dogs.

By the time I was grown, I had learned a lot about being a medicine man. My grandfather taught me how to worship the earth and how to make a sandpainting, collect herbs, and pray for people who are sick.

My grandfather was a Yeibichai dancer and taught me to be a Yeibichai dancer, too. The Yeibichai ceremony takes place during the fall harvest and is for a person who is sick all the time. The ceremony lasts for nine days. I learned other ceremonies as well and helped many people who were sick.

I really liked helping people get well, but it was a very hard job. People would come at all times of the day and night, wanting me to heal them. I would have to travel far from home for ceremonies, and I missed my family.

Being a medicine man is a serious job and takes a lifetime to learn. Not just anybody can be a medicine man. A medicine man must have much training and gain much knowledge from ancestors who were also medicine men.

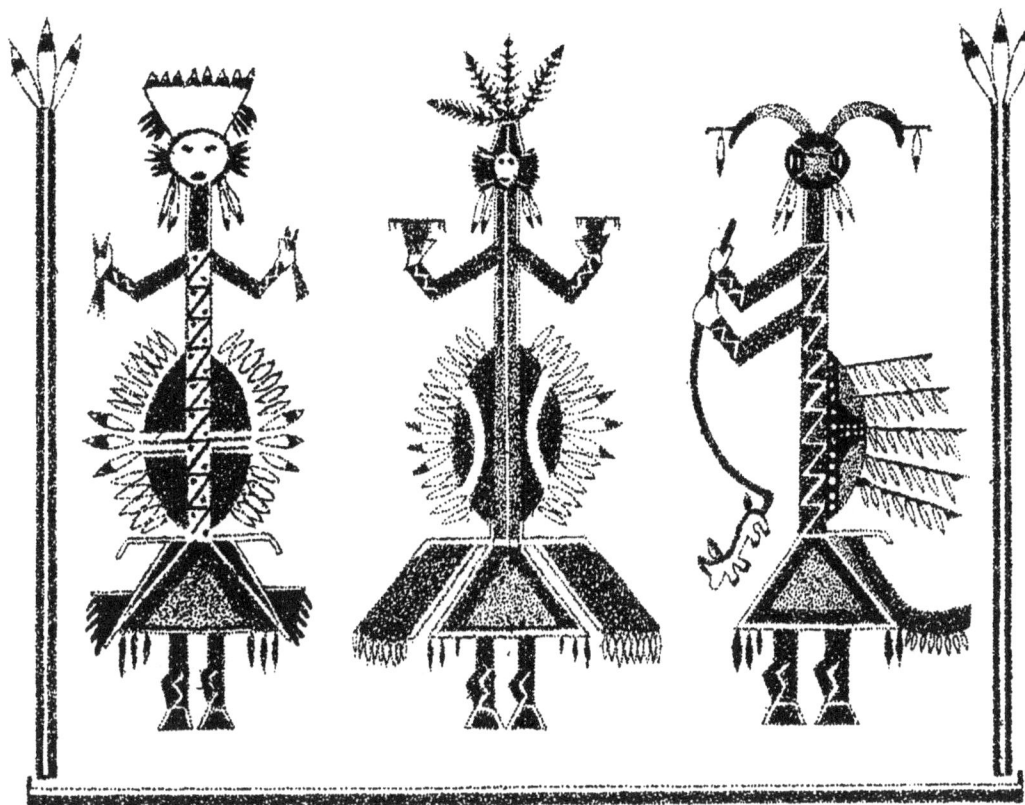

Exploring a Career as a Medicine Man

1. Discuss with the children how some careers are limited by the cultural knowledge and traditions required. As James explains, there are very few people who can become medicine men. They must have ancestors who pass down the gift and knowledge. For additional and intriguing information on James Joe and medicine men, read *James Joe: Autobiography of a Navajo Medicine Man,* by Susan Thompson (1996).

2. James Joe is known for his beautiful sandpaintings (see sandpainting of Yeibichai dancers, above). Sandpaintings are created during healing ceremonies, and different sandpainting designs contribute to the healing of various ailments. Many Native Americans create sandpaintings on boards, but these sandpaintings are never exactly the same as the ones used in religious ceremonies. Share a sandpainting or picture of a sandpainting with the children. It is not considered appropriate for non-Indians to create sandpaintings in the traditional designs because these sandpainting designs are for religious purposes, but children can still admire their beauty. The children can explore the process of gluing sand on boards in a design that represents something to them. A good book that has photographs of sandpaintings, explains the figures and designs in sandpaintings, and describes the techniques of sandpainting, is *Navajo Sandpainting Art,* by Eugene Baatsoslanii Joe (1978).

3. Take children to a museum in your area, or have books available so they can look at cultural artifacts from Navajo and other tribes. Talk with the children about the usefulness, beauty, and tradition of the various artifacts.

4. Children will enjoy reading other books that tell about the Navajo culture.

Chapter 31

Park Ranger

Interview With Larry McClenney

For eight years, I have been a National Park Service ranger. Philadelphia is a fascinating place in which to work for the Park Service. I meet with groups of children and adults, and I tell them about the Liberty Bell, the formation of the U.S. Constitution, and the legacy of Benjamin Franklin.

There are Park Service jobs all across the nation. Some jobs are in historical sites such as here at the Liberty Bell. Others are in natural environments such as the Grand Canyon. Many people begin working for the Park Service as volunteers. Some are in high school, and others, such as retired citizens, are older. To be paid as a Park Service employee, you have to have a minimum of a four-year college degree. It is very helpful if you know several languages because we hear people speaking about 30 different languages throughout the year.

I have always been interested in history, and I like meeting people and sharing information with them, so this is a good job for me. The people that I meet come from all over the world. It is very rewarding to help them learn about important historic events. This job also gives you a chance to develop confidence interacting with many groups of people.

Sometimes the job's hours are not all that convenient. We do work on weekends, and that takes us away from our families. But one big advantage is that you get to wear a uniform, so you never have to get up in the morning and wonder what to put on that day.

Exploring a Career With The Park Service

1. To help children better understand what Larry's job is, read them a book about the Liberty Bell and the history of the United States, including the signing of the Bill of Rights. Milton Meltzer's (1990) *The Bill of Rights: How We Got It and What It Means* will help children examine different laws and how they affect people today as well as present the history of the document.

2. Each child can practice being a park ranger. Help each child make a paper badge to pin on, with the words "Park Ranger" and then his or her name. The children can pick a historical event they would like to tell about. For example, a child may select to be a

park ranger at the Grand Canyon, Mesa Verde, or Ellis Island. Lead children in researching their places and help them prepare talks about the history of those places. Then each child can present a "tour" talk to the others about his or her selected area, as if he or she were a park ranger. For the talk, each child can prepare a visual or share a photograph from a pamphlet or book.

3. Put a map of the United States on the wall. What national, state, or local parks are in the state where the children live? Which parks are in surrounding states and other places in the country? Children should write to various parks to request information. Place pins in the map at the locations of the various parks contacted, and share the information obtained with all the children.

4. Larry says that he hears up to 30 languages throughout the year. If children were to go to a tourist attraction in their community, how many languages would they hear? What would the languages be? Talk with the children about the importance of knowing more than one language in any job that requires working with people from a variety of locations or backgrounds. What other jobs would this include? The children will probably mention store clerks (see candy clerk interview on page 31), bus drivers, pilots, and others.

NATIONAL PARK SERVICE

Department of the Interior

Chapter 32

Peace Corps Worker

Interview With Wendy Smith

The Peace Corps is a U.S. government-sponsored volunteer organization that sends people to places all over the world to provide medical, educational, and agricultural assistance. As a Peace Corps volunteer, my job was to work in a rural health center in South Korea, helping in tuberculosis control. Most of my time was spent visiting the homes of tuberculosis patients and trying to convince them to take all their medicine, every day. The medicine tasted bad, so most patients did not like to take it. I also went to public schools and spoke to children about how to prevent the spread of diseases like tuberculosis.

When I was in the third grade, I read in a *Weekly Reader* about the Peace Corps. It was a new organization then, started by President Kennedy. After reading about how many people were being helped around the world by their volunteers, I knew that I wanted to join when I was older.

Joining the Peace Corps was my dream, and I loved meeting so many people, learning another language, and learning about the Korean schools. I especially liked teaching children in the Korean schools about health education. In the Korean culture, people often sing songs for each other. When I went to speak in the Korean schools, the children often asked me to sing after I spoke. Although I don't sing very well, I enjoyed singing Korean songs for them. It helped them to see that I really respected their culture. I did miss my family since I was so far away from my home.

The Peace Corps has three basic goals:

1. To allow Americans to get to know another culture.
2. To allow people in the Peace Corps countries to get to know American culture.
3. To help developing countries in some way.

I learned that, even though the United States is more technologically advanced than many other countries, all people in the world have things they can teach us. Being a Peace Corps volunteer changed my life in many ways.

Exploring a Career as a Peace Corps Worker

1. Have a world map available for the children to examine. Where is South Korea on the map? Who are its neighbors? Do the children know of anyone who has traveled there? What can they find out about Korean culture and the people who live in North and South Korea? Explain to the children that South Korea is part of our global community. Younger children will be interested in knowing that children in South Korea go to school just as children in the United States do and that Korean children live in houses. Older children will be fascinated by the two Koreas' economic and political systems.

2. Talk with the children about what they can do to help other people. Some will help their families, others may help a neighbor doing yard work or other chores, and others may help in their communities. What gifts do they as individuals have that they can share with others? The gifts may be as simple as being kind to a smaller brother or sister or a sharing of time such as reading to an older person at a care facility. Brainstorm with children about different ways in which they can help people they know.

3. Explain to the children that part of being a good citizen is helping others. Help them organize schoolwide projects that can help others. The Christmas holiday season is a good time to contribute to structured projects such as collecting food to donate to the Salvation Army or bringing mittens and hats to hang on a Christmas tree. The mittens and hats can then be donated to children at their school or another school in the community.

   To help children contribute to a global community, they can participate with Life Care in preparing shoe boxes for needy children in war-torn countries. Have them bring in small gifts of toys, school supplies, and other supplies and put them in shoe boxes. The shoe boxes can then be wrapped by the children and mailed to other parts of the world through Life Care. Life Care collects over 50,000 shoe boxes each year to mail to children. (For more information about this program, contact a Life Care Center in your area.)

4. Children will be inspired to read about and hear from others who have contributed a great deal in terms of time and talents to other people in the world. Invite speakers from your community to talk about projects they are involved in that help others. Children can bring in newspaper and magazine articles about people who help others in a wide variety of ways.

5. There are many famous people who have spent their lives trying to make things better for other people. Mother Teresa is an excellent role model. Children will be inspired by *Mother Teresa: Sister to the Poor,* by Patricia Reilly Giff (1986).

6. Ask the children to pretend that they are applying to work with the Peace Corps. Have them write a practice letter to the Peace Corps organization expressing their interest and what they would like to accomplish. Where would they like to go? What work would they like to be involved in? What would they hope to accomplish?

   Merni Ingrassia Fitzgerald's (1986) *The Peace Corps Today* will provide them with good ideas about the Peace Corps and what they can do to help.

7. Talk with the children about helping others in other places. Explain to them that people learn as much from the people they are helping as those being helped learn from them. Each culture has wonderful things to share, and all people have talents and abilities from which others can learn. Wendy talks about this in the interview when she mentions how what she learned has helped her in many areas of her own life. Involve children in reflecting on a situation in which they learned something from another person and how it has helped them in their own lives.

Chapter 33

Piano Teacher

Interview With Gretchen Young

Music has always been a major part of my life. I started taking piano lessons when I was in kindergarten, and I always thought it would be fun to teach piano lessons when I was grown. In high school, I started teaching some lessons and decided to be a piano teacher.

I teach private and group lessons in my home. My students are all different ages—five years old through adults—and I teach them how to play the piano. They also learn the theory of music and music history and perform in recitals.

My favorite part of my job is teaching children. Since I have many of the same students year after year, I get to know them very well. It is very interesting to watch the students grow up and become better and better at playing the piano. When they graduate from high school, I think back to the boy or girl they were in kindergarten, and I am very proud of them. There is a bulletin board in my piano studio, and I put each child's picture on it. It's fun to know the children and to have them for friends. I also like working in my home and being my own boss.

About 35 students come to my home every week for their lessons. Because most of the students are in school, they come after school and in the evenings. This makes a long day for me and for my own children.

I learned how to teach piano by taking lessons, studying music in college, and practicing hard over the years. I also read music magazines and books and go to programs and workshops, all of which helps me become a better teacher.

Besides teaching lessons, I am the pianist at the Methodist Church, and sometimes I play the organ for special events such as weddings, programs, and funerals. I also like to write songs for children to play and sing and have published many of these in books for children. "I Am a Lump of Clay," on page 120, is a simple song I wrote. Teach the children the song. At the end of the song (after "what will I be?"), ask a child to act out something the clay might become. Each child can guess what the first child is acting out. After a child guesses correctly, sing the song again. The child who guessed correctly can then take a turn acting out what the clay may be. Continue the game and song until each child has had a turn.

I Am a Lump of Clay

I am a lump of clay, sit - ting on the floor;

Dream - ing of the day when I'll be a lump no more.

Some - one will pick me up, roll me and knead me;

Throw me on the ta - ble, tic - kle me and squeeze me.

What will I be?

Exploring a Career as a Musician

1. Play a musical tape for children that features a pianist. Explore with them their thoughts about the music and how the music makes them feel.

2. Talk with the children about famous musicians. Kathleen Krull's (1993) *Lives of the Musicians: Good Times, Bad Times (and What the Neighbors Thought)* is an interesting book that introduces children to various musicians and their fascinating lives.

3. Involve the children in writing a song of their own. They can take a simple tune, like the tune for "Old McDonald Had a Farm," and change the words. Or, for a good challenge, children can create musical instruments using household items. A pan with a wooden spoon makes a good drum. An empty juice can with rice or beans and a cardboard lid makes a good rattle. Encourage the children to create music from their household instruments that goes well with poems they have written or poems by others. They may also want to try to write a play or story, adding music at appropriate places. *Music, Music for Everyone,* by Vera B. Williams (1984), is a book about Rosa, a girl who created the Oak Street Band.

4. Explain to children that, like many careers, becoming a pianist takes a great deal of discipline and lots of practice. Explore with them things they are involved in that take a large commitment of time and energy, such as their participation in sports, dance, and art. Ask them to think about whether they would be willing to invest hours every day practicing to become very accomplished.

5. Share David Anderson's (1982) beautiful book *The Piano Makers* with the children. Talk with them about the artistry and skill that go into creating a piano.

Chapter 34

Postal Worker

Interview With Steve Rea

When I first began working for the post office, I was a mail clerk. Then I became a carrier and delivered mail to people's houses. It was an interesting job, and the people on my route would wait for me to come. They would take their mail and talk with me about a lot of interesting things. Through the rain, snow, wind, and hot weather, I would deliver the mail.

Now I work in the post office receiving and processing outgoing mail for delivery to post office boxes throughout the United States and around the world. When a person mails a letter (if in an outside box), it is brought to the post office in a truck. The mail is unloaded from the truck onto a conveyor belt, then dumped into a hopper, which empties onto another conveyer belt, where it is marked through a process that faces the mail all one way and cancels the stamps with the current date. There are many mail handlers who work at the conveyor belt and sort out the larger pieces of mail.

Then the mail is loaded into trays and weighed. After this, it is placed on a shaker table, which shakes the mail and makes it even for the machine. The machine reads the delivery address (if it is typewritten) and then "sprays" a bar code onto each envelope. The bar code is then used to sort the mail into a different bin for each state in the United States.

If an envelope is handwritten, the machine will reject it, and it goes into a different bin. This mail is read by postal clerks and sorted into the correct bin. Canadian and other foreign mail is routed to a bin requiring additional handling by other postal workers.

The machine that sorts the mail is 90 feet long, and 600 pieces of mail can be processed in a minute; or 36,000 letters an hour. The letters go through so quickly that you can hardly tell they are letters. When the letters (or large envelopes) have been sorted by state from bins into trays labeled by zip codes, they are wrapped together by an automatic strapper. The tray is weighed on a machine called a scanner and assigned a number code. The number code determines how the mail will be delivered. Some mail is delivered by a truck and other mail by airplane.

Our busiest time of year is around Christmas. Also, at the beginning of each month, we get a lot of mail from people paying their bills. On an average day, we receive 80,000 to 90,000 pieces of mail. On a busy day, we receive 120,000 to 130,000 pieces of mail, and during the Christmas season, we have up to 200,000 pieces of mail each day!

The work I do can be dangerous because the conveyor belt and other moving parts on the machinery move at extremely high rates of speed. Thus, safety is a major concern. The rules and regulations are strictly enforced. There can be no loose-fitting clothes, no jewelry, and long hair must be tied up. There are STOP buttons/switches located every three feet in case of an emergency.

There is a lot of satisfaction in knowing that a postal clerk's work helps people stay in touch. What would the world be like without mail? People write to businesses, stay in touch with their loved ones, and even stay connected to men and women who are overseas in the military service.

Exploring a Career as a Postal Worker

1. Involve children in practicing writing letters and addressing them to their friends and family. Talk with them about the importance of the zip code and where it belongs on the envelope. Have each child tell the others where his or her letter is destined. With the children, find the location on a map and point out where that letter will end up when it reaches its final destination. *Postal Workers A to Z,* by Jean Johnson (1987), is an enjoyable story for primary-grade children, following a piece of mail until it is delivered; and children of all ages will enjoy Harold Roth's (1983) *First Class!: The Postal System in Action.*

2. A wonderful literacy play center can be developed in one corner of the room. Children can play "postal worker" and "post office" at this drama center. Stock the center with large strapped bags with which to carry mail, envelopes and paper, pencils and other writing tools, a stamp to use in canceling the mail, books about the post office, and other props. They can actually "mail" their letters at their post office, and designated mail carriers can deliver them to children in the room and in other rooms in the school.

3. Visiting a post office is a fascinating field trip. Everyone will be impressed by the volume of mail that goes through a post office, whether in a small town or in a large city. Have children observe how many workers are in a post office and record all the different jobs they do.

4. Steve works for the United States Postal Service. Talk with the children about other ways that mail is delivered. Have they ever received a package from United Parcel Service or Federal Express? Discuss with them when people may want to use UPS or FedEx.

5. How do we know how much postage to put on a letter or package? Explain to the children that the amount of postage needed depends on the weight of the letter or package. For normal delivery, a letter of one ounce or less requires a 34-cent stamp (as of March 2001). If possible, have a scale available for them to weigh their letters. How much does one of their letters weigh? How many stamps will it need? How about a small box or a cardboard tube?

6. Talk with children about the history of mail delivery in this country. The Pony Express is one example of how mail was delivered in the western United States during one period. The children will be interested in how the mail was delivered by people riding horses. Steven Kroll's (1996) *Pony Express!* brings this history alive for children. Have them think about how far we have come from the Pony Express to the mail process Steve describes. What advantages and disadvantages do they see in the modern process and in delivering mail by horse? They may mention that the machinery can break down and that horses can become sick and tired. The modern process helps mail go around the world where horses cannot travel.

Chapter 35

Prison Teacher and Director

Interview With Rich Mendenhall

There are numerous jobs in a prison. People cook food, clean, do the laundry, and check out books. Others are security guards, full-time dentists and doctors, and some even work in a prison pharmacy. There are teachers in a prison, and I am one of them. I also supervise other teachers who teach some prisoners basic reading and writing so they can earn a high school equivalency diploma, learn carpentry, plumbing, computer work, horticulture, and interior renovation. These are all areas in which they can find jobs or that will provide them with hobbies when they get out of prison.

Helping people gives me a very real sense of accomplishment. I love to teach and give someone a skill or trade that will help in his or her life. I listen to people a lot and try to help them, and sometimes I get really tired because it's hard to help everyone with what they need.

The prison I work in is in Ohio. The people I work with are interesting. Some try very hard, and some do not. There is a lot of variety in what I teach and the people I teach. I had to go to school and become certified as a teacher to teach any GED (General Education Degree) course. To teach a vocational class like carpentry, you need to have a minimum of five years of experience and a vocational certificate.

I feel safe working in the prison. There are many guards and a lot of structure, so I know what to expect. The prisoners are incarcerated for a variety of crimes. I try to get to know them as people and not think about the crimes they have committed. Many of the prisoners can learn new things that will help them to be successful in the outside world.

Exploring a Career Working in a Prison

1. Talk with children about prisons and the goal of prisons, which is to rehabilitate. Many children will be surprised by Rich's interview and will not realize that some prisoners have many opportunities while they are incarcerated. Ask them how they think learning a trade or to read and write will make a difference for a prisoner when he or she leaves the prison.

2. Rich and other instructors teach many different things to the prisoners. Some teach carpentry, others reading, and some even gardening. What other things would be interesting and helpful for the men and women at the prison to learn? What skills do prisoners need to make a living when they get out of prison? What hobbies might they want to learn to enrich their lives?

3. Explain that some people take a GED test instead of earning a high school diploma. There are practice books available for the GED that children may want to examine to see the types of things adults are expected to know to pass the GED. Also talk with them about different people who need help learning basic skills so they can be successful on this test, such as people who have not been able to go on in school, those for whom English is a second language, and teenagers who have had trouble graduating from high school. Explain that many communities have teachers to help students learn so they can pass the GED.

4. Talk about the other jobs that Rich mentions people do in a prison. Help the children compare a prison's needs to the needs of other places where large numbers of people stay, such as hotels or hospitals. Why would prisons need librarians, laundry help, doctors, and dentists?

5. Freedom is very valuable. Workers in the prison get to go home at night, whereas the prisoners do not. Explore the concept of democracy with the children. Explain that with certain rights there are certain responsibilities. One of the responsibilities each person has is to obey the law. Talk about the rules in the library, classroom, or school. Why are these rules important? Caroline Arnold's (1983) *Why Do We Have Rules?* explores some of these basic concepts. What would happen if the rules were not followed (people would get hurt, property would be destroyed, etc.)? People working in prisons who are not prisoners often think about freedom because they spend their days with people who do not have the freedoms they have.

Chapter 36

River Trip Guide

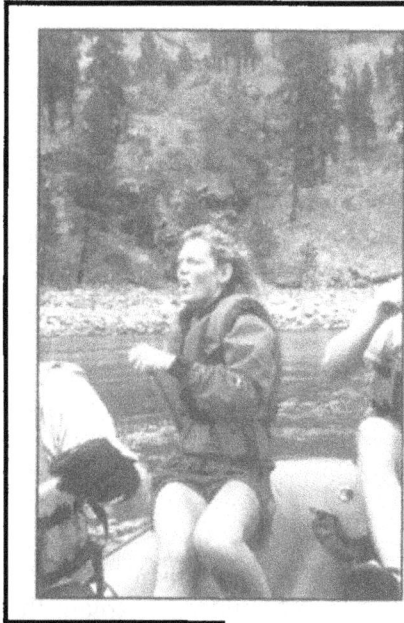

Interview With Sara Clement

I love river rafting. I am a river guide on the Main and Middle Fork of the Salmon River near Salmon, Idaho. Between three and six guides take 15 to 25 guests on five-day river trips. As a guide, I get up at 5:30 or 6:00 every morning to cook breakfast. We also make lunches and dinners for the guests. I learned to make delicious chocolate cake in a Dutch oven. After breakfast, we clean up camp, load the boats, and row all day. We stop for lunch, row some more, and then set up camp around 4:00 in the afternoon. We play games with the guests or let them rest until we cook dinner each night. After dinner, we tell stories by the campfire, sing, and, on the last night of each week, we have a talent show in which everyone participates.

When I was young, maybe in junior high school, I decided that I didn't want to look back on my life and think, "I could have done that" or "I wish I would've done that." I wanted to live life fully and to try everything. I'd much rather say I tried and failed than that I never tried at all. So I made a dream list. One of my dreams was to dance on a roof in London; another was to be a river guide. I wanted to see a sunset in Africa, and I wanted to win a dance competition. These aren't my main goals in life—these are dreams, things I think about when my mind wanders. I have more serious goals about the person I want to become and what I want to do in other aspects of my life, but for me, the dreams are just as important.

I'm surprised, too, at how many of my dreams have come true. I did dance on a roof in London, I am a river guide, and I won a swing dance competition. Now, I've begun a list of dreams accomplished, and I'm always adding to my dream list.

I love my job because I love people, being in the sun, camping, water, and adventure. I remember waking up early one morning just after dawn. I looked around at the river, the mountains on either side, and the yellowish sky. I thought to myself, "I can't believe I get paid for this job." I never wear a watch. I never know if it is Monday or Tuesday because it doesn't matter. We keep track of days by the food we serve. For example, day one is steak night, and day four is fajitas.

I feel alive on the river in a way that I never have before. I use my body every day—sometimes to the point of exhaustion, and then I learn to keep going past that point. Some senses that don't get used in everyday life are the most important on the river. I feel so in tune with myself and with nature on the river.

I also love working with people. I meet people from all over the world and become friends with them in the course of the week when they are on the river. It has opened my world view, and I have learned to accept differences and appreciate all kinds of people. I love river rafting because I feel like I am living life fully. My boss hired all of the guides based on our personalities. He said he hired people who would work well together and then he trained us. Before I was a river guide, I was a swim teacher and lifeguard, so I already had experience in the water. Verle, our boss, takes all the new guides up to the Main Salmon before the season starts, and we run the river in two days, three times. For example, we run the whole five-day trip in two days, then we drive back around to Salmon and do the river again the next day. So in one week, we run the whole river (over 95 miles) three times. After that, we have our licenses to run the river and just keep doing it every week all summer long.

I love river rafting. It changed my life and challenges me physically, emotionally, and mentally in ways I would never have experienced if I hadn't been a guide. Because I am a guide, I'm pretty sure I can do anything if I put my mind to it. Next summer, I'm going to be an ice-climbing guide in Juneau, Alaska, on the Mendehall glacier near Glacier Bay National Park.

Following is a piece I wrote about feeling afraid to be a guide when I was just learning.

My Experience Being Trained as a River Trip Guide

I look at the eight guests, including my dad, who are looking at me. I see the other three gear boats upstream.

"Verle," I shout, "What do I do?"

"Row hard and catch the next eddy, 'cause after Jim Moore's cabin, Whiplash is around the corner." He doesn't look back when he answers. He and another guide, Heather, are already stroking, leaving us behind.

Whiplash is a huge rapid. I need to pull into the eddy ahead and not go right into Whiplash. Get to the side of the river, Sara, I coach myself. Row hard! Pull, pull! I half grunt, straining from the weight of the overloaded boat. Each time I pull, my legs tense, and I use my whole body to stroke. Hit the wave straight, pull through. There's the eddy; go for it. I'm tired; my strokes lose strength. I want to cry, to scream, to let my dad take over the oars.

Verle and Heather make it to the eddy. I'm pulling, stroking, and pulling. We're not making it. I look back at Verle; we are 10 feet from each other. He is in the eddy, and I am not. Whiplash is near, and I am not ready to run through this rapid. I look into his eyes.

"Don't you give up, Sara, pull," he mouths or shouts, I'm not sure which. For Verle, I pull. Fear turns to anger, adrenaline, and I pull. The people in my boat say things to encourage me; I see their mouths move, but I do not hear them. Pull, Sara. Pull, pull, pull! The repetition inside my head keeps my strokes steady.

We make it to the eddy, and I'm exhausted. I put the oars under my knees to hold them in place. I let my arms rest and my head sag toward my chest. The people in my gear boat cheer while I concentrate on breathing and wipe sweat from my forehead.

I look up to see Verle. He smiles, nods his head in approval, and says, "Nice rowing." I smile and stand up. Verle's compliment gives me confidence.

I start to leave, and my dad gives me a hug. "Wow, kid," he says, "good job. It was hard to see my girl work so hard and not be able to do anything. I wanted to take the oars from you."

"Don't you dare, Dad. This is my job," I answer in a serious tone because I want him to understand that he can't protect me. He has to be more of a guest than a dad on this trip. "Besides," I add, "I'm a licensed river guide." We both laugh because I've been certified for less than a week.

Exploring a Career as a River Guide

1. Ask the children to name and describe different water sports. Many children will be swimmers, some will play water polo, and others may canoe or water ski. How about other outdoor sports like ice climbing, bicycling, and hiking? Encourage them to share experiences they have had with various outdoor sports.

2. Sara has to think creatively and carefully about what to cook on a camp stove for a group of people. With the children, plan and cook a meal on a camp stove. Talk with them about what can or cannot be cooked easily. Explain that a one-dish meal is easiest because it can be cooked in one pan. For example, hash brown potatoes from a box with melted cheese on top would be easy to prepare, as would spaghetti with bottled sauce. Also, help them think about what can be carried easily in a cooler on the river. Fresh fruits, vegetables, and meat will not keep for very long. Then involve children in preparing the meal on the camp stove and tasting their camp-cooked dinner.

3. In Sara's short story, she describes being afraid to run the river. Talk with the children about times in their lives when they were afraid to try something and then conquered their fears, such as learning to ride a bike. They can illustrate their experiences on drawing paper, using crayons, colored pencils, or paints.

4. What would you pack if you went on a river trip for one week? How about a camping trip to the mountains or desert? What would you need in terms of shelter, drink, food, and clothing? How about insect repellent and other items? The children can make a list of all the things that they might take. After the lists are completed, involve them in looking back over the items listed and thinking about which items are really necessary for survival and which are not. They can cross out the items not absolutely necessary, discussing each item with other group members as they sort through the list.

5. The children can investigate more about river sports by reading *Canoeing,* by Celeste A. Koon (1982), and *River Thrill Sports,* by Andrew David and Tom Moran (1983). For an introductory book on kayaking, suggest Bill Lund's (1996) *Kayaking.*

6. Sara tells about her dream list. All of us have things we dream of doing. Ask the children to create dream lists and share their dreams with a friend.

Chapter 37

Secretary

Interview With Susan Ray

When I was a young girl, I loved to play like I was working in an office. I also liked to play "school." Now I am a secretary in a program that teaches people to be elementary teachers, and I have the best of both worlds.

There are about 100 adult students in our teacher education program who are learning how to be elementary teachers. I am the secretary of our program. I help all of our students check out books and video cameras, work with the computers, and answer questions they may have. I enjoy supporting the students as they learn and grow to be the best teachers that they can be. The students in our program are kind and helpful to one another. Over the years, I have made many friends, and I must be a good listener because even when they become elementary teachers, they still come back and tell me all about what they are doing.

I also help the teachers in our program be the best that they can be. They ask me to help them prepare materials to teach with, order books for their classes, and help coordinate appointments and program activities.

In our program, we have a lot of special events. For example, we hosted a "Read Across America" celebration. A lot of children came with their parents to read books. When we have these types of events, I make flyers advertising them and help organize the events.

These are just some of the things I do. A secretary usually helps everyone around him or her in any way he or she can. Your school secretary probably helps all of you in many ways.

I took classes in high school that helped me learn how to be a secretary, such as typing and bookkeeping. After high school, I went to college and studied data processing. Most of what I do as a secretary I learned on the job. My job has changed a lot over the years. When I first became a secretary, there were no computers to work on, and we had to type everything. Computers really changed people's jobs and made them much easier in some ways.

Exploring a Career as a Secretary

1. Set up a secretary play literacy center. Include file folders to be labeled, a computer, books, telephone, paper, and pencils. The children can practice the jobs that secretaries do while at the same time increasing their own literacy skills by labeling materials, writing letters, filing folders in alphabetical order, and so forth.

2. Have different children take turns being the class secretary. Involve the class secretary in taking minutes, arranging the books in the class library, mailing letters to parents, and doing other jobs that resemble jobs a secretary would normally handle.

3. Some children in the class may want to "job shadow" with the actual school secretary. They will be surprised at the variety of jobs a secretary does during the day and at the knowledge the school secretary has about all aspects of the school and the families that come to the school. Have the children that are "job shadowing" keep notes on all the secretary's duties during the period they are with him or her and report back to the class.

4. When some employers interview for secretarial positions, they will have the person being interviewed answer the telephone to hear how polite he or she is and to listen to what he or she says. It's very important for a secretary to have good telephone skills because the secretary represents the place of business and this is the first impression that the person calling has of the business. Have two play or real telephones available for the children to practice with. Have them take turns placing a call to a place of business, and have other children take turns being the secretary who answers the telephone. Does the "secretary" provide the caller with appropriate information, and is he or she polite to the caller?

5. The children can practice developing a flyer that advertises some real or imaginary event. What information will need to be included in the flyer? What font or print style will be attractive? Will the flyer include pictures? What colors will be best for the flyer?

6. Teach the children a standard format for a business letter. Florence D. Mischel (1957) provides good information for children on writing letters in *How to Write a Letter*. Involve the children in selecting a business or person to whom they would like to write to request some information. Help them write and mail the letter. Allow time for them to share the responses they receive.

Chapter 38

Sheepherder

Interview With Tom Rogers

My name is Tom Rogers, and I am a sheepherder on the Pitchfork Ranch near Laramie, Wyoming. I have herded sheep all my life. I am a Navajo Indian, and I grew up in Arizona. My family raised goats and sheep, and I helped with the herding when I was a little boy. We lived in a hogan and burned firewood when we wanted to cook our food and for heating our home.

My life is lonely. I watch sheep all day long, making sure that they stay together in a flock and do not wander off. During the day, I have to push sheep down from the hills so they stay with the group. "Shaggy Bear" is my sheep dog, and he helps me round up the sheep. I herd sheep during May, June, July, August, and September.

On a typical day, I get up at 6:00 in the morning and check the sheep, then go into the wagon and make some breakfast. After breakfast, I water the sheep at a nearby watering hole. At noon, I eat lunch and then watch the sheep in the afternoon. At night, I eat supper and sleep in my sheep wagon.

Exploring a Career as a Sheepherder

1. Involve the children in writing about the following: If they came upon a sheep wagon and saw the sheepherder sitting against a tree, with his sheep dog lying at his feet, what could they ask him? These could be questions such as, "What do you do all day?" and "What do the sheep eat?"

2. Read the following newspaper advertisement for a sheepherder to the children. Discuss the job expectations and salary.

    SHEEPHERDER: With minimum of 30 days' experience. Attends sheep grazing on range, herds sheep using trained dogs. Guards flock from predators and from eating poisonous plants. May assist in lambing, docking, and shearing. Large flocks with a single-pair herder. Food, housing, tools, supplies, and equipment provided. Hours variable, on call 24 hours 7 days. Terms of employment from 11 mos. up to 3 years. Employment for 3/4 of workdays guaranteed. Transportation to job and subsistence advanced. Employment available in several western states including: NV, AZ, CA, OR, ID, WA, CO, WY, UT. Min. salary is $650 to $851; salary varies according to state. Contact: State Employment, Casper, WY.

3. As indicated in the advertisement, some sheepherders also shear the sheep. The sheep are shorn in the spring. With the thick wool off their bodies, the sheep can nurse their babies more easily. Also, their coats can grow back before winter. Each sheep grows about 30 pounds of wool that covers its body. When the wool is shorn, each sheep's wool is called a "fleece." The wool is packed into bags. Remind the children of the nursery rhyme:

    Black sheep, black sheep,
    have you any wool?
    Yes sir, yes sir,
    Three bags full.
    One for my master,
    One for my dame.
    And one for the little boy
    Who lives down the lane.

    Three bags full is a lot of wool. Each bag holds about 300 pounds!

    On page 137 is a depiction of a rancher "jumping the bag" as he fills a bag with newly shorn wool.

4. Have some shorn wool for the children to examine. Wool can be purchased directly from ranchers or from local weavers. Involve the children in pulling the wool apart. What happens? The wool "sticks" together as you pull because of many tiny scales in each wool fiber. Examine a fiber under a microscope and look at how the tiny scales overlap each other. A wool fiber has a wavy shape and will stretch because it is elastic. Let the children stretch a fiber and see how it returns very slowly to its original length and shape. That's why their wool clothing will smooth itself out after being hung to dry.

5. Wool has a distinct feel and odor of oil. Have the children smell the wool. See whether they can feel the oil. Talk about why the wool has such an oily consistency. The oil is called "lanolin" and is used in cosmetics and ointments. Suggest to the children that they look at the grocery store for other products that use lanolin.

6. Pass around garments made from wool, such as socks and sweaters. Explain that wool clothing is the warmest natural-fiber clothing we can wear. Wool absorbs moisture from the surrounding air and yet still feels dry. It keeps the moisture away from your skin, keeps the heat of your body from escaping into the air, and keeps you warm.

7. There are advertisements for sheepshearers in various newspapers in the United States. The following advertisement is from a newspaper in Casper, Wyoming. Read the advertisement to the children and lead them in discussing what it would be like to shear sheep for a living. What special skills and talents are needed to be a sheep shearer?

Sheep Shearers Wanted: Applicants should have sufficient experience to shear by using power-driven clippers; 96–125 ewes per day after a 5-day break-in period. Applicants w/hand shearing experience only and who are able to shear at a rate of at least 70 ewes per day must be given the opportunity to adapt to use of power-driven clippers. Must be willing to shear w/o tying the feet when that is required by woolgrowers. Will be given the opportunity to learn to shear loose. Place in a shearing station, clip wool close to hide so wool is removed in one piece. Exercise care not to nick, pink, or cut skin and to avoid double cuts. May help move sheep in and out of shearing area. Oils hand tools and sharpens combs and cutters. May tie fleece. Perform all job-related duties according to employer requirements. Will work in dust, cold, snow, etc. Wages: $1.50/head w/own equip. $1.45/head w/o own equip. Transportation and subsistence expenses to work site will be reimbursed by employer upon completion of 50% of the work contract from job, if contract is completed. Tools and equipment provided w/o cost to worker, if applicable. Free housing provided. Duration: 1/11/99 to 5/20/99.

8. Sheepherders of long ago are thought to have worn a special watch that told time by the sun. A simple band for telling time can be made out of thick paper. Have the children cut strips of paper that will wrap around their wrists like a bracelet (see drawing on page 138). On the inside of one end, they should ink in the times and grid (see drawing). On the end of the other side, they need to punch a hole through the bracelet. When the sun shines through the hole, it will indicate the time on the grid. (For daylight saving time, add one hour.)

9. A good book to share with children about a Navajo sheepherder is *Little Herder in Autumn,* by Ann Nolan Clark (1988), and interesting books about Navajo weaving are *The Goat in the Rug: As Told to Charles L. Blood and Martin Link*, by Charles L. Blood (1976) and *Annie and the Old One,* by Miska Miles (1971).

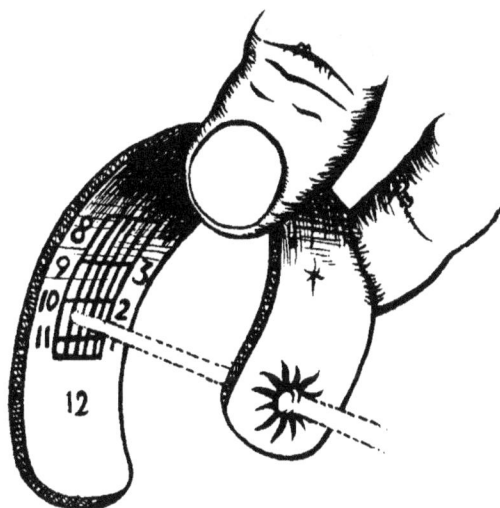

Chapter 39

Shiprock Trading Post Clerks

Interviews With Maxine Begay and Rosita Yazzie

My name is Maxine Begay, and I work with my friend Rosita Yazzie at the Shiprock Trading Post, which is on the Navajo Indian Reservation in Shiprock, New Mexico. A trading post is like a store where people bring things they or their families have made, and they sell them to us or trade them for other things in the store. It used to be that people on the reservation would bring in pieces of their artwork such as turquoise jewelry, rugs, and baskets to trade for food, blankets, and other supplies. Now we pay them for their art, and they buy things with the money.

Many people come to our trading post to buy the artwork that we have purchased from Navajo Indians who live in this area. It was hard to learn about all the art. We had to talk with a lot of people and read about the designs, materials, and history of each type of art. For example, with the rugs, we have to know who wove the rugs, the cultural understandings, and what the colors represent.

We ship pieces of artwork all over the world, and we travel to about five shows a year where we show and sell pieces of artwork. When orders come in that need to be mailed out, we have to be careful to wrap the items carefully so they do not break. For example, the pottery and kachina dolls have to be wrapped in styrofoam packing peanuts to be well protected.

Working in a trading post is a very interesting job. You get to look at lots of beautiful art and meet such interesting people. You can challenge yourself and try to make some of the art that you see. Rosita wove a rug with a two grey hills pattern a little while ago and sold it here. She really felt good to create a rug and have someone buy it—that was satisfying.

Exploring a Career as a Trading Post Clerk

1. Explain to the children that in the past, people used to barter for goods and services. For example, if one person could shoe a horse well but could not hunt well, he might shoe a horse in trade for meat. The idea of the original trading post was that of trading one thing for another. Have each child think of something that he or she can do well that is a service someone might need, then draw a large symbol representing this talent on a piece of paper. A child who bakes well might draw a batch of cookies, and one who knows how to canoe may draw a boat. When they are finished with their drawings, each child can hold up the drawing and look around at what he or she would like to trade for. After the children have traded services, allow time for discussing the process of trading goods.

2. Discuss the responsibilities that Maxine and Rosita have as store clerks in the Shiprock Trading Post. They have to learn all about what they are selling and be very careful about how they wrap items for shipping. Provide the children with styrofoam peanuts, shredded paper, cardboard boxes, and breakable items such as bowls and vases to practice wrapping for shipping. Demonstrate, or have someone from a shipping service demonstrate, how to wrap a fragile item so that it can be shipped safely without breaking.

3. An excellent book about trading posts on the Navajo Reservation is *Trading Post Guidebook,* by Patrick Eddington and Susan Makov (1995). Children will be interested in the goods that have been traded at trading posts and are still traded today. Trading posts can be very isolated in canyon country where most of them exist. To gain a better understanding of the history of rugs found in trading posts, read *Annie and the Old One,* by Miska Miles (1971), to the children.

4. Involve children in discussing today's society and whether it would be practical today to trade goods. How would a barter system affect the way we live in the United States? What would happen to our grocery stores? What advantages and disadvantages can the children think of?

5. If we went into a trading post, we could tell a lot about the people who live in the area by what they trade. Ask each child to bring something personal from home that he or she might be willing to trade if he or she needed to trade for goods. (Reassure the children that they will have their items returned.) Put the items in the middle of the room and position the children so they are in a circle surrounding the items. What do the items tell the group about themselves as a whole? What items represent their talents, interests, and living requirements?

The illustration below shows supplies of sand, glue, and boards, which can be purchased at some trading posts for making sandpaintings. See Chapter 30 for more information about sandpainting.

Chapter 40

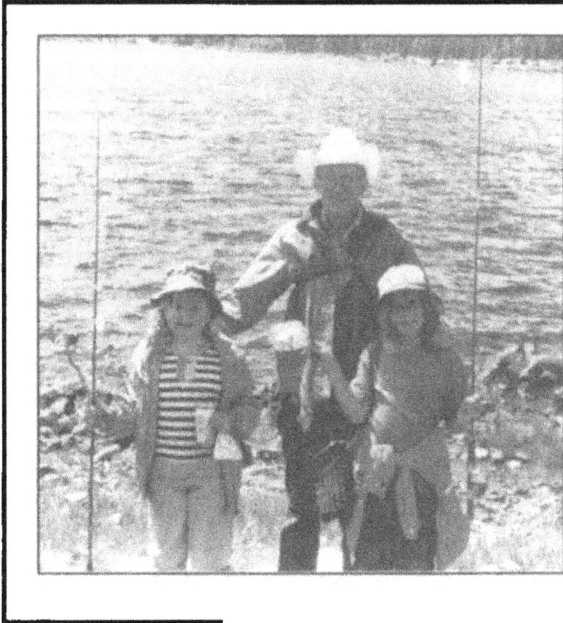

Superintendent of Schools

Interview With William Conklin

I like three things very much: I like being around children, I like the many wonderful people I meet being a superintendent of schools, and I enjoy the feeling of accomplishing something very worthwhile with my life: the education of children.

I started out in education as a junior high school teacher. After several years, I went back to school and received a doctoral degree in school administration and became a superintendent of schools. To be a superintendent of schools, a person must have teaching experience and at least a master's degree in school administration. A superintendent of schools is a busy person.

A superintendent must make many decisions, big and small, every day. I am responsible for giving leadership to the school district and to make sure that the policies and regulations of the school board are carried out in the district. I also recommend policies to the board and keep the community aware of the students' needs and accomplishments.

The most important elements in a school district are the children and the teachers teaching them. But for teaching and learning to occur, a lot of other things have to be provided. These include books you use in school, books for the library, and other student supplies; the curriculum—what is taught at each grade level and how it is taught; finances—the money needed to buy supplies, pay salaries, clean buildings, run school buses, hire teachers and other employees; providing good school buildings; and keeping the parents and other adults informed about the school district and how well students are learning.

The superintendent has many people to help him or her do his or her job, and it is important that they all work together as a team.

The most important thing is to have an excellent school system so boys and girls are happy, safe, engaged in what they are learning, and learning a lot. I love to visit the classrooms and think it is fun to sit down with students at a reading table and listen to them read. It's great to see how much students improve from the first of the year to the last day of the year. Being with students is really the best part of the job.

Being a superintendent takes a lot of time, and the job is not just Monday through Friday during the day. There is often a lot of night and Saturday work attending meetings and student activities, and planning the next day. And then there are those early morning snowstorms—deciding whether to close school.

Sometimes it's hard to satisfy everybody involved in certain situations because they may have different viewpoints, but this is a challenge and not really a disadvantage. Part of leadership is working out the best solution to problems in such a way that no one becomes angry even though there may be strong disagreements regarding the solution.

Exploring a Career as a Superintendent of Schools

1. Explain to the children that the superintendent is actually the leader of the schools. Together, after reading Superintendent Conklin's interview, look around the room and talk about what the superintendent is responsible for in schools: the books the children read, the desks or tables they sit at, the teacher who teaches them, even the bus they ride to school. Explore the concept of leadership and explain that a leader is responsible for many things that happen in an organization. As a group, brainstorm about other community leaders such as the mayor, a local legislator, or a religious figure. James A. Eichner and Linda M. Shields (1964) explore community leadership in *Local Government.*

2. Each child can draw a picture of a school bus on paper, using crayons. Have each child include himself or herself in the picture, looking out of a window. Explain that how the students come to school and everything that happens at school are part of the superintendent's job responsibilities. Talk with the children about the difficulties of a job in which a person is responsible for so many decisions. For example, in deciding whether to close school based on the weather, the superintendent has to find out how the roads and weather will affect the buses and all the children and their families, then decide what is best for all. Have the children reflect on a time when they made an important decision that affected others. What decision did they make, and how did they decide what would be best?

3. Involve the children in thinking about something they value in their school or school district and guide them in painting a mural representing their ideas, using paints or crayons. The mural can be labeled "Schools allow me to . . ." Talk with them about what is important to them in their schools, and connect their values with what they can accomplish for others as a teacher or public school administrator. For example, some children may represent reading books or being involved in learning new things through science experiments. Talk to them about how, if they were teachers or administrators, they could adopt new reading programs, purchase supplies for science experiments, and involve families in reading and science activities.

4. Who else makes decisions besides the superintendent? With the children, chart the decisionmakers in the school district and their relationship with one another. List the teachers, the school board members, the superintendent, the assistant superintendent(s), the principal, and so forth. Talk about the jobs and responsibilities each has. Who else has jobs in a school district? The school district personnel also include cooks, custodians, bus drivers, secretaries, and substitute teachers.

5. Children will be interested in thinking about how schools have changed over the years and how a teacher's or public school administrator's job has changed. An interesting book on the history of schools is *Historic Communities: A One-Room School,* by Bobbie Kalman (1994). This book covers everything from how children used to travel to school, to running the school, the daily routine, and even games played at school.

Chapter 41

Truck Driver

Interview With Doug Watkins

Everything you have eaten and worn today—the fuel in your car, and even your toothpaste and stuffed animal—was transported to stores on trucks. Many people don't realize what is carried in trucks. There used to be a lot of refrigerated train cars carrying produce, but now most is carried in trucks. People want produce like broccoli at all times of the year, and they can have it because of the refrigerator trucks. Or apples, for example, are stored at a temperature that puts them to "sleep" for months at a time and then they can be shipped to grocery stores during all times of the year. Our grandmothers used to can a lot of their fruits and vegetables, but now we store them and then ship them through the winter.

I learned to be a truck driver ten years ago. There was a guy I started learning from who drove with me all over the country. It was really an on-the-job type of training. I watched him drive for about a day, and then I was the main driver.

Big companies have established routes and drivers. Their drivers usually know where they are going and how long they'll be gone. I own my own truck, and I'm an independent driver. Companies call me when they want me to haul a load.

It's a good job because I'm a paid tourist. I get to see every part of the country. There are times when I get to request a place. I say, "Hey, find me a load to Florida." My mother lives in Texas, so I say, "Find a load in Dallas." I pull a refrigerator car, which keeps produce cool in the summer and warm in the winter. I carry my motel right with me. Sleepers are nice on the trucks. They have a TV, refrigerator, bed, and even reading lights.

Being a trucker is a lonely job though. You have to be able to get along with just yourself. In the summer, I travel at night and sleep during the day because at night there are not so many tourists and other traffic on the road. The trucking companies are starting to train husband and wife teams so they can keep each other company. My wife, Cathy, used to go on trips with me. I have a daughter who is going to be in second grade, and next year I will get to take her on some long trips.

There are times when truck drivers are very helpful on the road. One time, when I was on the road, I saw a lady school bus driver who was not paying attention take a curve too fast and tipped the bus over. There was other traffic coming that would also hit the bus. A truck driver who was behind the bus positioned his truck and trailer across the exit to block the traffic. It turned out that he had a wife who was a nurse, and he had helped her study so he also knew quite a bit of first aid and was able to help a lot of the kids. I also was on the scene and helped direct traffic.

Many truck drivers and schools participate in a program called "Trucking Buddies." The kids really love the program, and so do many truckers. I was a trucker buddy. As a trucker buddy, I would be part of an elementary classroom, telling them about my travels. When I would pick up a load, I would send an interesting postcard telling where I was and what load I had on board. The kids would love hearing from me and kept track of where I was traveling with a map on a bulletin board. They were surprised to see how fast I would go across the country. One friend of mine is a trucking buddy, and one time he washed and shined his truck up really nice and took it to school when he was traveling through their town. It was fun for him to meet the kids, and they enjoyed meeting him and seeing his truck. To get a trucking buddy, you can call **1-800-MYBUDDY**, or go to *truckerbuddy.org* on the Internet. Kenworth, a maker of trucks, works with the buddy program.

Exploring a Career as a Truck Driver

1. Ask the children to think about the items that Doug talks about hauling. What types of categories are there? The categories include produce (fruits and vegetables), toys, clothing, and household items. Look at pictures of and read about various trucks in books such as *The Truck Book,* by Rick Sensbach (1991), and *Trucks and Trucking,* by Ruth Wolverton and Mike Wolverton (1982). Talk with the children about how different trucks are designed to carry different loads. Doug's current truck is designed for produce as well as dry goods. His first trailer was a flatbed trailer for hauling pipe, lumber, and brick. What kind of truck would you need for gas and oil?

2. Have the children make small trucks out of school milk cartons stapled onto quart milk cartons. They can paint them or cover them with colored paper. Wheels can be made from firm paper or cardboard and glued onto the body of the truck. The children can cut out the back end of the carton along the bottom and sides to create a flap that closes. Out of small boxes, construction paper, and other materials, they can create items to place in the truck. Where is the truck going, and what is it carrying? Challenge the children to create a writing (maybe even a poem) about their truck's journey and share it with other children.

3. Become part of the Trucker Buddy program. Mount a map on a bulletin board, and as your trucker travels and sends mail, draw the route with a marker across the map. Attach yarn to the letters or postcards. Pin the other end of the yarn to the locations from which the mail was sent. What does your buddy haul? Where is he or she taking the produce or other goods? Is he or she picking up produce or other goods at a certain location? Is this where the produce is grown or the goods are made? What else can you find out from your buddy?

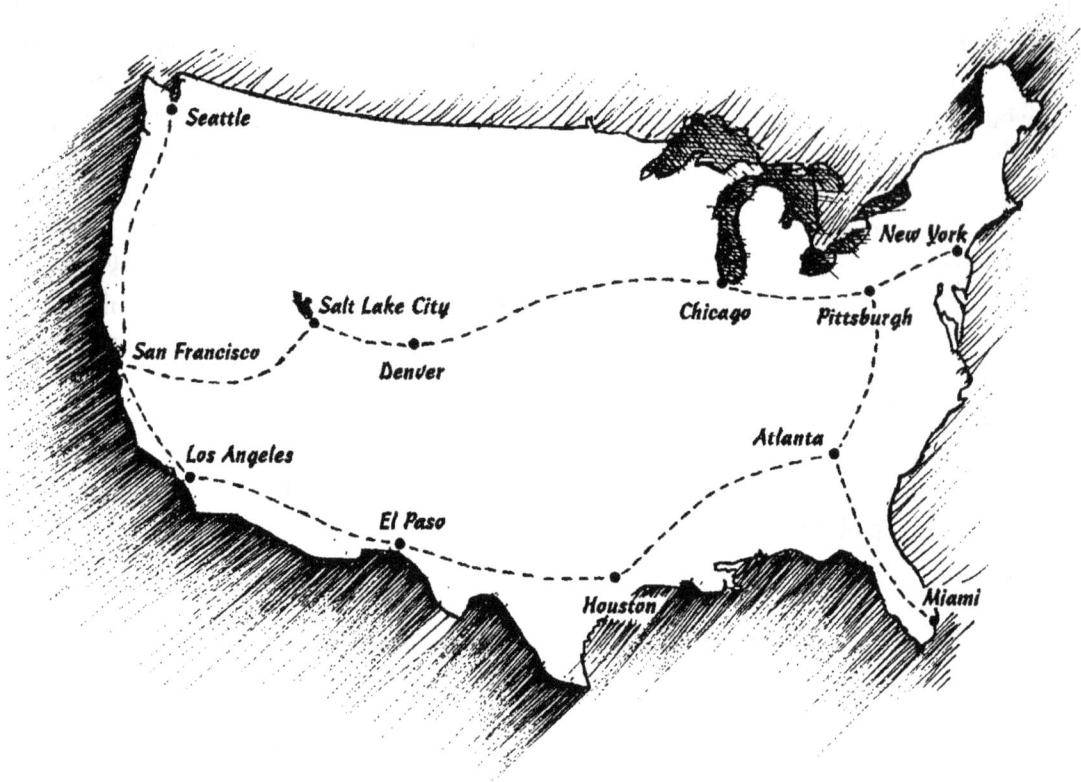

4. Talk with the children about how important it is for a trucker to drive safely. The trucks are big, and there are many on the road. What are some of the traffic laws the drivers must pay attention to? In addition to speed limits, there are many signs that children will be interested in learning about and discussing. The signs that are commonly seen by children are ones that tell drivers to stop, yield, and turn or not turn on red lights; yellow lights for caution; and ones indicating that lanes will merge. Talk with them about signs and other markings on roads that tell whether you can safely pass a car. The children will be interested in other signs and markings around their school, such as crosswalks, handicapped parking areas, and areas where buses stop. Talk with them about the different signs and help them recognize and learn new signs by looking at signs in a traffic manual or in a children's book such as *I Read Signs*, by Tana Hoban (1983).

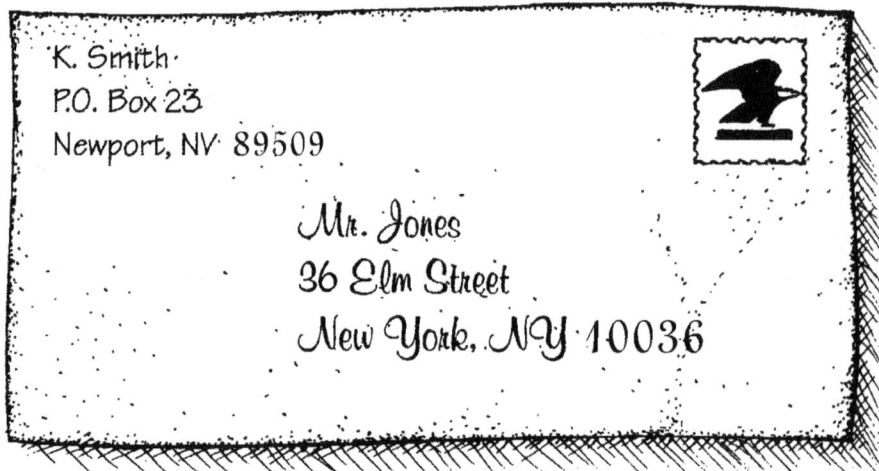

K. Smith
P.O. Box 23
Newport, NV 89509

Mr. Jones
36 Elm Street
New York, NY 10036

Chapter 42

Weaver

Interview With Maximina Lopez

My mother taught me to weave when I was seven years old, and I taught my daughters to weave the brightly colored and beautiful weavings. We live in San Antonio Aguas Calientes, a small village in Central America, at the base of a volcano. We are Mayan, and we speak Cakchiquel and Spanish, and my older daughter is learning to speak English.

We weave on a backstrap loom. This is a loom that goes around a person's waist. It takes a lot of skill and care to weave the fine threads into cloth. The designs I weave are in my head, taught to me by my mother. The weaving takes a lot of time—weeks or even months—but I like being an artist. My work is beautiful, and many people buy and enjoy my weavings. If the threads are light in color, I can weave at night in the moonlight, but if the threads are darker, I weave during the day at my shop.

My shop is on a cobblestone street in Antigua, Guatemala, and I go there every morning on the bus. Sometimes my daughters go with me. They also weave colorful wall hangings to sell to tourists and other people who come into the shop. During the day, we laugh and talk about all that goes on. At the end of each long day, we get back on the bus and ride home to our house at the base of the volcano.

Exploring a Career as a Weaver

1. Show the children various woven articles of clothing or photographs in books of weavings. Discuss the differences in the weaves—wool being much bulkier than fabrics woven with thread, like those of Maximina's. Explain to them that although Maximina weaves with a backstrap loom, many women in Guatemala weave on machine looms in factories.

2. Discuss the interview with Maximina. Her village is built on the Agua Volcano, *agua* being the Spanish word for water. Although the volcano is active, it has been a long time since its last eruption. On page 152 is an illustration of the village of Antigua, where she travels each day to share her goods.

3. Other weavers in Antigua, where Maximina's shop is, carry their weavings in large bundles on their heads. They carry them to the marketplace to sell to tourists and other people. Carrying a large bundle on a person's head is a skill or talent in itself. Ask the children to try to walk with a book balanced on their heads. Can they wrap many towels or other fabrics into a big bundle and balance it on their heads while they walk? See illustration on the next page. For an interesting book on markets, see Ted Lewin's (1996) *Market*.

4. It takes Maximina many weeks, and sometimes months, to make one of her beautiful weavings. She sells most of them for less than $10.00 each. That is not very much money in our country, but it is quite a bit in Guatemala, where the average yearly income for a family of four is equal to about $600 in U.S. currency. It's important that children start developing a global understanding of people and how varied their lives are. A wonderful book that takes the reader to places around the world is *Material World: A Global Family Portrait,* by Peter Menzel (1994). The book introduces readers to families from all areas of the world. At each location introduced, a family is in its yard, in front of its home, along with all the material goods it owns. Children will be fascinated as well as surprised at how different families live, and in many cases, how few material goods they own.

5. Weaving is a commonality that every culture throughout the world shares. Throughout history, people in every culture have woven cloth. Children can experiment with weaving by hand. Young children can learn the patterns of weaving in and out using paper strips, or even using a plastic loom with loops that are commonly sold on which to create potholders. Older children may want to weave on dried twigs from trees or on a small wood loom. Loom patterns are in *Folk Art Tells a Story,* by Susan Conklin Thompson (1998). Camilla Gryski's (1993) *Friendship Bracelets* instructs children on how to weave the colorful friendship bracelets commonly found in Mexico, Guatemala, and other parts of the world.

6. Clay work—bowls, pots, and statues—is another craft that we all share historically. *World Crafts: A Celebration of Designs and Skills,* by Jacqueline Herald (1992), introduces children to the crafts that we find throughout the world, weaving as well as many others, from making clay pots to carving on gourds. Other books that tell about traditional crafts and provide information for creating them include *Handmade Tiles,* by Frank Giorgini (1994); *Decorative Mosaics,* by Elaine M. Goodwin (1992); *Papercrafts: 50 Extraordinary Gifts and Projects,* by Gillian Souter (1994); and *The Complete Candlemaker: Techniques, Projects, and Illustrations,* by Norma J. Coney (1997).

7. *Abuela's Weave,* by Omar S. Castañeda (1993), tells a story about a girl and her grandmother who weave on a backstrap loom in Central America. The children will enjoy this story as well as *The Most Beautiful Place in the World,* by Ann Cameron (1988), which gives an additional glimpse into Mayan life. For an overview of Guatemala, children may want to read *Guatemala,* by Sean Sheehan (1998); *Guatemala: Central America's Living Past,* by Lila Perl (1982); and *A Life of Their Own: An Indian Family in Latin America,* by Aylette Jenness and Lisa W. Kroeber (1975).

8. The designs Maximina weaves come from her memory. She has learned them from her ancestors. Explain that it is difficult to repeat a design on both sides of a rug. Challenge children to take a piece of white paper and pretend that it is a weaving they are creating. Using paints or crayons, they can create small paper rugs of their own. If children want to use graph paper, they can make a design that is more mathematically precise.

References

Aardema, Verna. *Bringing the Rain to Kapiti Plain.* New York: Dial Press, 1981.

Aliki. *Fossils Tell of Long Ago.* Rev. ed. New York: Thomas Y. Crowell, 1990.

————. *Marianthe's Story: Spoken Memories/Painted Words.* New York: Greenwillow Books, 1998.

Ancona, George, and Joan Anderson. *The American Family Farm.* Orlando, Fla.: Harcourt Brace Jovanovich, 1989.

Anderson, David. *The Piano Makers.* New York: Pantheon Books, 1982.

Anno, Mitsumasa. *Anno's Flea Market.* New York: Philomel, 1984.

Armstrong, William H. *Barefoot in the Grass: The Story of Grandma Moses.* Garden City, N.Y.: Doubleday, 1970.

Arnold, Caroline. *Why Do We Have Rules?* New York: Franklin Watts, 1983.

Aylesworth, Jim. *County Crossing.* New York: Atheneum, 1991.

Blood, Charles L. *The Goat in the Rug: As Told to Charles L. Blood and Martin Link by Geraldine.* New York: Aladdin Books, 1976.

Blumenson, John J.-G. *Identifying American Architecture.* New York: W. W. Norton, 1977.

Branley, Franklyn M. *Water for the World.* New York: Thomas Y. Crowell, 1982.

Cameron, Ann. *The Most Beautiful Place in the World.* New York: Random House, 1988.

Carle, Eric. *Walter the Baker.* New York: Simon & Schuster, 1972.

Carroll, Colleen. *How Artists See People: Boy Girl Man Woman.* New York: Abbeville, 1996.

————. *How Artists See Weather: Sun Wind Snow Rain.* New York: Abbeville, 1996.

Castañeda, Omar S. *Abuela's Weave.* New York: Lee & Low Books, 1993.

Chalmers, Margaret Taylor. *Colonial Fireplace Cooking & Early American Recipes.* East Lansing, Mich.: Eberly Press, 1979.

Clark, Ann Nolan. *Little Herder in Autumn.* Santa Fe, N.Mex.: Ancient City Press, 1988.

Cole, Joanna. *Cuts, Breaks, Bruises, and Burns: How Your Body Heals.* New York: Thomas Y. Crowell, 1985.

Cole, Joanna, and Stephanie Calmenson. *Marbles: 101 Ways to Play.* New York: William Morrow, 1998.

Coney, Norma J. *The Complete Candlemaker: Techniques, Projects, and Inspirations.* Asheville, N.C.: Lark Books, 1997.

Cosner, Shaaron. *Special Effects in Movies and TV.* New York: Simon & Schuster, 1985.

David, Andrew, and Tom Moran. *River Thrill Sports.* Minneapolis: Lerner, 1983.

Dubrovin, Vivian. *Storytelling for the Fun of It: A Handbook for Children.* Masonville, Colo.: Storycraft, 1994.

Eddington, Patrick, and Susan Makov. *Trading Post Guidebook.* Flagstaff, Ariz.: Northland, 1995.

Eichner, James A., and Linda M. Shields. *Local Government.* 2nd rev. ed. New York: Franklin Watts, 1964.

Field, Rachel. *General Store.* Boston: Little, Brown, 1988.

Fitzgerald, Merni Ingrassia. *The Peace Corps Today.* New York: Dodd, Mead, 1986.

Fortney, Mary T. *Fire Station Number 4: The Daily Life of Firefighters.* Minneapolis: Carolrhoda Books, 1998.

Garaway, Margaret Kahn. *The Old Hogan.* Tucson, Ariz.: Old Hogan, 1993.

Gibbons, Gail. *Check It Out! The Book about Libraries.* San Diego: Harcourt Brace Jovanovich, 1985.

———. *Farming.* New York: Holiday House, 1988.

———. *How a House Is Built.* New York: Holiday House, 1990.

———. *Lights! Camera! Action!: How a Movie Is Made.* New York: Crowell, 1985.

Giblin, James Cross. *Let There Be Light: A Book about Windows.* New York: Thomas Y. Crowell, 1988.

Giff, Patricia Reilly. *Mother Teresa: Sister to the Poor.* New York: Viking Penguin, 1986.

Giorgini, Frank. *Handmade Tiles.* Asheville, N.C.: Lark Books, 1994.

Goodwin, Elaine M. *Decorative Mosaics.* New York: Henry Holt, 1992.

Graff, Nancy Price. *The Strength of the Hills: A Portrait of a Family Farm.* Boston: Little, Brown, 1989.

Greene, Ellin. *Clever Cooks: A Concoction of Stories, Charms, Recipes and Riddles.* New York: Lothrop, Lee & Shepard, 1973.

Gryski, Camilla. *Friendship Bracelets.* New York: William Morrow, 1993.

Herald, Jacqueline. *World Crafts: A Celebration of Designs and Skills.* London: Charles Letts, 1992.

Hoban, Tana. *I Read Signs.* New York: William Morrow, 1983.

Hobbs, Will. *Far North.* New York: Morrow Junior Books, 1996.

———. *Howling Hill.* New York: Morrow Junior Books, 1998.

Jenness, Aylette, and Lisa W. Kroeber. *A Life of Their Own: An Indian Family in Latin America.* New York: Thomas Y. Crowell, 1975.

Joe, Eugene Baatsoslanii. *Navajo Sandpainting Art.* Tucson, Ariz.: Treasure Chest Publications, 1978.

Johnson, Jean. *Postal Workers A to Z.* New York: Walker, 1987.

Kalman, Bobbie. *Historic Communities: Games from Long Ago.* New York: Crabtree, 1995.

————. *Historic Communities: Home Crafts.* New York: Crabtree, 1990.

————. *Historic Communities: A One-Room School.* New York: Crabtree, 1994.

Kalman, Bobbie, and David Schimpky. *Historic Communities: Old-Time Toys.* New York: Crabtree, 1995.

Kehoe, Michael. *The Puzzle of Books.* Minneapolis: Carolrhoda Books, 1982.

Klein, Norma. *Baryshnikov's Nutcracker.* New York: G. P. Putnam's Sons, 1983.

Klutz. *Nail Art.* Palo Alto, Calif.: Klutz, 1997.

Knight, Margy Burns. *Welcoming Babies.* Garner, Maine: Tilbury House, 1994.

Koon, Celeste A. *Canoeing.* New York: Harvey House, 1982.

Kroll, Steven. *Pony Express!* New York: Scholastic, 1996.

Krull, Kathleen. *Lives of the Musicians: Good Times, Bad Times (and What the Neighbors Thought).* Orlando, Fla.: Harcourt Brace Jovanovich, 1993.

Kuklin, Susan. *Fighting Fires.* New York: Macmillan, 1993.

Lasky, Kathryn. *Puppeteer.* New York: Macmillan, 1985.

————. *Sugaring Time.* New York: Macmillan, 1983.

Latham, Jean Lee. *Elizabeth Blackwell: Pioneer Woman Doctor.* Champaign, Ill.: Garrard, 1975.

Lewin, Ted. *Market.* New York: Lothrop, Lee & Shepard, 1996.

Lindblom, Steven. *How to Build a Robot.* New York: Thomas Y. Crowell, 1985.

Lund, Bill. *Kayaking.* Mankato, Minn.: Capstone Press, 1996.

Mabery, D. L. *Tell Me about Yourself: How to Interview Anyone from Your Friends to Famous People.* Minneapolis: Lerner Publications, 1985.

Martin, Beryl. *Batik for Beginners.* Sydney: Angus and Robertson, 1971.

McGovern, Ann. *If You Lived in Colonial Times.* New York: Scholastic, 1964.

Meltzer, Milton. *The Bill of Rights: How We Got It and What It Means.* New York: Thomas Y. Crowell, 1990.

Menzel, Peter. *Material World: A Global Family Portrait.* San Francisco: Sierra Club Books, 1994.

Miles, Miska. *Annie and the Old One.* Boston: Little, Brown, 1971.

Mischel, Florence D. *How to Write a Letter.* 2nd ed. New York: Franklin Watts, 1957.

Munro, Roxie, and Julie Cummins. *The Inside-Outside Book of Libraries.* New York: Childrens Books, 1996.

Oneal, Zibby. *Grandma Moses: Painter of Rural America.* New York: Viking Penguin, 1986.

Pallotta, Jerry, and Rob Bolster. *Going Lobstering.* Watertown, Mass.: Charlesbridge, 1990.

Perl, Lila. *Guatemala: Central America's Living Past.* New York: William Morrow, 1982.

Phillips, Betty Lou. *Brush up on Hair Care.* New York: Mesner, 1982.

Polacco, Patricia. *The Trees of the Dancing Goats.* New York: Simon & Schuster, 1996.

Pringle, Laurence. *Natural Fire: Its Ecology in Forests.* New York: William Morrow, 1979.

Rabott, Ernest. *Frederic Remington.* New York: HarperCollins, 1988.

Rockwell, Anne. *The Storm.* New York: Hyperion Books for Children, 1994.

Roop, Peter, and Connie Roop. *Keep the Lights Burning, Abbie.* Minneapolis: Carolrhoda Books, 1985.

Rosenak, Chuck, and Jan Rosenak. *The People Speak: Navajo Folk Art.* Flagstaff, Ariz.: Northland, 1994.

Rosenberg, Jane. *Dance Me a Story: Twelve Tales from the Classic Ballets.* New York: Thames and Hudson, 1985.

Rosenberg, Liz. *Monster Mama.* New York: Putnam, 1993.

Ross, Laura. *Finger Puppets: Easy to Make, Fun to Use.* New York: Lothrop, Lee & Shepard, 1971.

Roth, Harold. *First Class!: The Postal System in Action.* New York: Pantheon Books, 1983.

San Souci, Robert D. *Feathertop: Based on the Tale by Nathaniel Hawthorne.* New York: Doubleday Dell, 1992.

Sandomir, Larry. *Isadora Duncan: Revolutionary Dancer.* Austin, Tex.: Steck-Vaughn, 1995.

Saul, Wendy. *Butcher, Baker, Cabinetmaker: Photographs of Women at Work.* New York: Thomas Y. Crowell, 1978.

Saunders, Susan. *Margaret Mead: The World Was Her Family.* New York: Viking Penguin, 1987.

Schiffer, Nancy N. *Navajo Arts and Crafts.* West Chester, Penn.: Schiffer, 1991.

Schwartz, Alvin. *Stores.* New York: Macmillan, 1977.

Selden, Bernice. *The Mill Girls.* New York: Atheneum, 1983.

Sensbach, Rick. *The Truck Book.* Fairfield, N.J.: Horowitz/Rae, Itasca, 1991.

Sewall, Marcia. *People of the Breaking Day.* New York: Macmillan, 1990.

Sheehan, Sean. *Guatemala.* New York: Marshall Cavendish, 1998.

Siebert, Diane. *Train Song.* New York: Thomas Y. Crowell, 1981.

Simon, Norma. *All Kinds of Families.* Morton Grove, Ill.: Albert Whitman, 1976.

Simon, Seymour. *A Building on Your Street.* New York: Holiday House, 1973.

———. *New Questions and Answers about Dinosaurs.* New York: William Morrow, 1990.

Sobol, Harriet Langsam. *Clowns.* New York: Coward McCann & Geoghegan, 1982.

Souter, Gillian. *Papercrafts: 50 Extraordinary Gifts and Projects, Step by Step.* New York: Crown Trade Paperbacks, 1994.

Spier, Peter. *People.* New York: Doubleday, 1980.

Thompson, Susan. *James Joe: Autobiography of a Navajo Medicine Man.* Billings, Mont.: Council for Indian Education, 1996.

Thompson, Susan Conklin. *Folk Art Tells a Story: An Activity Guide.* Englewood, Colo.: Libraries Unlimited, 1998.

U.S. Department of the Interior, National Park Service, Division of Publications. *Lowell: The Story of an Industrial City.* Washington, D.C.: Government Printing Office, 1992.

Venezia, Mike. *Van Gogh.* Chicago: Childrens Press, 1988.

Wandro, Mark, and Joani Blank. *My Daddy Is a Nurse.* Reading, Mass.: Addison-Wesley, 1981.

Ward, Alan. *Machines at Work.* New York: Franklin Watts, 1993.

Warren, Lee. *The Dance of Africa: An Introduction.* Englewood Cliffs, N.J.: Prentice-Hall, 1972.

Wiggers, Raymond. *The Amateur Geologist: Explorations and Investigations.* New York: Franklin Watts, 1993.

Wilder, Laura Ingalls. *The Little House on the Prairie.* New York: Harper, 1953.

Wilkinson, Beth. *Coping with the Dangers of Tattooing, Body Piercing, and Branding.* New York: Rosen, 1998.

———. *Papermaking for Kids: Simple Steps to Handcrafted Paper.* Layton, Utah: Gibbs Smith, 1997.

Williams, Vera B. *Music, Music for Everyone.* New York: Mulberry Books, 1984.

Winter, Jeanette. *Diego.* New York: Alfred A. Knopf, 1991.

———. *My Name Is Georgia.* Orlando, Fla.: Harcourt Brace, 1998.

Wolverton, Ruth, and Mike Wolverton. *Trucks and Trucking.* New York: Franklin Watts, 1982.

Writer's Digest Books. *Writer's Market.* Cincinnati: F & W Publications, 1998.

Yolen, Jane. *Owl Moon.* New York: Philomel Books, 1987.

Young, Sue. *Writing with Style.* New York: Scholastic, 1997.

Zoehfeld, Kathleen Weidner. *How Mountains Are Made.* New York: HarperCollins, 1995.

Index

About the Author

Author Susan Thompson (right) with Jean Schieck, the baker featured in Chapter 5.

Susan Thompson, Ed.D., began her career in education as a second-grade teacher in the mining community of Hanna, Wyoming. She is currently an associate professor of education and director of elementary education programs for the University of Wyoming Casper College Center. Susan loves meeting new people and enjoys friendships with many individuals who have various careers in different parts of the world. Susan has shared many creative ideas through the books she has written, which include *Hooray for Clay!, Natural Materials, Elephants Are Wrinkly,* and *Folk Art Tells A Story.* She has also written a children's book, *James Joe: Autobiography of a Navajo Medicine Man,* published by the Council of Indian Education. Susan lives with two daughters, Kayenta and Rosalie, and her husband, Keith, who is a geologist. All of them love to travel, meet new people, and learn about other people's jobs and careers.

from *Teacher Ideas Press*

GLUES, BREWS, AND GOOS
Recipes and Formulas for Almost Any Classroom Project
Diana F. Marks

You've got to have it! This indispensable activity book pulls together hundreds of practical, easy recipes and formulas for classroom projects. From paints and salt map mixtures to volcanic action formulas, these kid-tested projects make learning authentic and enjoyable. All projects use ingredients that are easy to find and processes that are up-to-date. **Grades K–6.**
xvi, 179p. 8½x11 paper ISBN 1-56308-362-0

SCIENCE THROUGH CHILDREN'S LITERATURE, 2d Edition
Carol M. Butzow and John W. Butzow

The Butzows' groundbreaking, critically acclaimed, and best-selling resource has been thoroughly revised and updated with new titles and new activities for today's classroom. More than 30 exciting instructional units integrate all areas of the curriculum and serve as models to educators at all levels. Adopted as a supplementary text in schools of education nationwide, this resource features outstanding children's fiction books that are rich in scientific concepts yet equally well known for their strong story lines and universal appeal. **Grades K–3.**
xix, 205p. 8½x11 paper ISBN 1-56308-651-4

MULTICULTURAL FOLKTALES
Readers Theatre for Elementary Students
Suzanne I. Barchers

Introduce your students to other countries and cultures through these engaging readers theatre scripts based upon traditional folk and fairy tales. Representing more than 30 countries and regions, the 40 reproducible scripts are accompanied by presentation suggestions and recommendations for props and delivery. **Grades 1–5.**
xxi, 188p. 8½x11 paper ISBN 1-56308-760-X

SUPER SIMPLE STORYTELLING
A Can-Do Guide for Every Classroom, Every Day
Kendall Haven

Aside from guides to more than 40 powerful storytelling exercises, you'll find the Golden List of what an audience really needs from storytelling, a proven, step-by-step system for successfully learning and remembering a story, and the Great-Amazing-Never-Fail Safety Net to prevent storytelling disasters. This system has been successfully used by more than 15,000 educators across the country. **All Levels.**
xxvii, 229p. 8½x11 paper ISBN 1-56308-681-6

MORE SOCIAL STUDIES THROUGH CHILDREN'S LITERATURE
An Integrated Approach
Anthony D. Fredericks

These dynamic literature-based activities will help you energize the social studies curriculum and implement national and state standards. Each of these 33 units offers book summaries, social studies topic areas, critical thinking questions, and dozens of easy-to-do activities for every grade level. The author also gives practical guidelines for integrating literature across the curriculum, lists of Web sites useful in social studies classes, and annotated bibliographies of related resources. **Grades K–5.**
xix, 225p. 8½x11 paper ISBN 1-56308-761-8

For a free catalog or to place an order, please contact:
Teacher Ideas Press • **Dept. B050** • **P.O. Box 6633** • **Englewood, CO** • **80155-6633**
800-237-6124 • **www.lu.com/tip** • **Fax: 303-220-8843**

www.ingramcontent.com/pod-product-compliance
Lightning Source LLC
Chambersburg PA
CBHW080550220326

41599CB00032B/6429